AMERICAN HISTORY

SUDOKU

TRIVIA
Volume-1

KURTIS M. WILLIAMS

TABLE OF CONTENTS

AMERICAN HISTORY SUDOKU TRIVIA PUZZLES INSTRUCTIONS

Welcome to an exciting NEW way of solving Sudoku puzzles! The <u>American History Sudoku Trivia Word Puzzle-Part 1</u> contains 152 puzzles, with trivia questions that reveal the clue word needed to solve each Sudoku puzzle using a combination of numbers and letters. By solving the trivia question, you reveal the 9-letter word used to solve the puzzle (hint – the clue word may be the combination of two or more words contained in the trivia question). The 9x9 grids are pre-filled with some of the clue word letters or numbers. Using logic and reason, fill in the remaining blanks, which will then reveal the clue word either vertically, horizontally, or backwards once in each puzzle. Each column and row must contain one each of the nine letters of the clue word, and each 3x3 grid the same. The puzzles span American history from the birth of the country to modern times. Some will be obvious while others will challenge your recollections of junior high history class! Don't let that deter you.

The Plateau people lived in rugged lands and did not raise crops but lived in small fish villages and hunted buffalo in ___ _____ of Oregon and Washington and Southeastern British Columbia.

	S		P	A				N
	A	I	T	N			S	E
		S		E	L			A
	E		H	I		N		P
I		P	N		L	S		H
N		H		A	T		L	
P		E	T		I			
S	I		A	L	H	P		
H			E	S		I		

Clue Word _ _ _ _ _ _ _ _ _

Puzzle # 1

What year marks the birth of the United States of America as an independent nation? This year was the _____ __ __.

S		O	H		B			
I		B		T				S
F		R	I		S	B	U	H
	B	H	U					O
O		U	F		H	S		T
T					R	H	B	
B	R	T	S		F	U		I
U				R		T		F
		T			O	R		B

Clue Word _ _ _ _ _ _ _ _ _

Puzzle # 2

When did Christopher Columbus arrive on the shores of America? And what was it called?

		Y	E	V	D		C	O
O			S		Y	D		E
	S	E	R					V
R			V	E				Y
		V	Y		I	E		
Y				R	C			I
S		R			E	O	V	
E			O	D		V		C
V	D			C	O	R	Y	

Clue Word _ _ _ _ _ _ _ _ _

Puzzle # 3

	E	H	X	U				A
S	U				T		M	
X	A	M				T		U
U	H			H	E	L		T
			S	M	L			
M	S	E	E				A	X
E		A		T		U	T	L
	T		A				E	M
L				E	U	A	X	

An urban center of the Mayas, run by ___ _____ about A.D. 925 to A.D. 1500.

Clue Word _ _ _ _ _ _ _ _ _

Puzzle # 4

I		Z	T					D
	A		C	I		E	N	
	Z	K						C
N	K		I		Z		D	
A	C						I	K
	E		N		C		Z	T
Z						T	E	
	I	E		Z	N		K	
K				E	A			I

These people in A.D. 1200 left large stepped pyramids, erected and built temples, used complex calenders, kept records, and sculpted images of their gods. Its priests carried the practice of human sacrifice to the extreme.

Clue Word _ _ _ _ _ _ _ _ _

Puzzle # 5

These people came into the region around Cuzco, in present-day "Peru" about A.D. 1250.

S			A	E				R
	R	E			N			
A	U	N				C	E	S
	N		I			A	C	P
		A				U		
E	P	S			C		N	
N	A	U				P	R	C
			C			S	I	
I				N	P			A

Clue Word _ _ _ _ _ _ _ _ _

Puzzle # 6

Spanish term for "My villages." This name is applied to groups of Native Americans because they were living in villages when the Spaniards arrived.

	M	B	U	L			I
S			B	O	E		
	P		M		I	L	E
	U		S			P	
L	S					E	U
		P			L		M
B		U	L		S		I
		O	E	B			L
P				M	U	O	S

Clue Word _ _ _ _ _ _ _ _

Puzzle # 7

The Incas today would be named this, as these people of "today" because of where they resided in A.D. 1250.

E	A	R		P			
			I	S	U		A
	S	U	R	A	E		N
S	R		A		P	E	
P							A
		V	N		R		P	U
	V		U	R	A	P	E	
	E		P	N	I		
				Y		I	U	N

Clue Word _ _ _ _ _ _ _ _

Puzzle # 8

	G		N		A	D		O
A				G	D	S		H
		H	S	U	M		A	
		A	H		G			D
		O				G		
N			A		O	H		
	O		G	M	N	A		
U		M	D	A				S
G			D	U		S		H

This tribe, in A.D. 1200, built what was upright and eight-sided structures of earth and wood near Pueblo settlements.

Clue Word _ _ _ _ _ _ _ _ _

Puzzle # 9

A people of about 700 B.C. built large earth mounds in the Mississippi River's valley. Some of the mounds contained burials and artifacts. These groups were _ _____ part of the "Creeks," Choctaws, Chickasaws, and Seminoles.

H	N	A		S				E
	U	O	R			T	N	
	T		N			H		
		S			O		E	N
			R					H
T	R		A			S		
E		R			U		H	
		N			Z	E	A	
				A			A	O	S

Clue Word _ _ _ _ _ _ _ _ _

Puzzle # 10

This tribe, rather than settling down, would __ _____. They were famously known as "The Apache."

	M	N	A	D				I
		B		I	A	E		
I		O						N
	B		I		N		O	
D		O	M		B	C		A
	E		C		D			
N					O			D
	I	M	D		C			
O				I	A	E	M	

Clue Word _ _ _ _ _ _ _ _ _

Puzzle # 11

I					H	T		U
N				G		H	I	
H		R	I					
	I	H	B	T		U	E	G
	E			I			H	
B	N	U		H	G	I	R	
				E	G			I
	H	T		B				N
G		I	N					H

Woodland culture peoples of the upper Great Lakes region harvested wild rice. "Menominee," which means white rice people, were also ___ _____ of wild buffalo and were named "The Iroquois."

Clue Word _ _ _ _ _ _ _ _ _

Puzzle # 12

The best-known Native Americans are those of the plains. Their native feather headdresses, their skill on horseback, and their bravery as fighters made them famous all over the world. Plains people such as these inhabited a large territory between the Mississippi River and the Rocky Mountains and were known as ___ _____.

		D		S				O
	T	A	M		N	D		
	S			A	O			N
		H	D	E	N			M
M								H
H		D	N	T	M			
E			A	M			S	
		H	S		D	A	N	
A			E		H			

Clue Word _ _ _ _ _ _ _ _ _

Puzzle # 13

Small nomadic bands of Utes, Paiutes, and Shoshones lived in the barren region between the Rockies and the Sierra Nevada. This area, shaped like a giant dish, included Utah, Nevada, and Eastern California. Food was scarce. This region was known as a ____ _____ because food was difficult to find.

		W			K	B	S	
		N	W	A	B			
		K	I	N				W
		A	R		O		I	S
N			S		A			B
I	O		B		N	R		
K				O	I	S		
			K	B	R	W		
	A	O	N			I		

Clue Word _ _ _ _ _ _ _ _ _

Puzzle # 14

_____ ____ _ was a very special culture along the Northern Pacific's stretched & narrow region of western Oregon, Washington, and British Columbia. The Tlingits in the north and the Chinooks in the south.

O			T	I	R		E	I
E	I		N				R	
T			H	W	E			
				N	I	E		
H		I				I		O
		O	W	H				
			R	O				N
	O						W	E
I	N		I	E				H

Clue Word _ _ _ _ _ _ _ _ _

Puzzle # 15

	S	T	H		M		A	
A	M			T			H	
	E	H	A		S		M	U
							H	E
		E		S		M		
U	T							
E	U		T		A	H	P	
	P			E			U	T
	H		M		U	A	E	

One of many small tribes among the Modocs and Pomos—Inhabited the coastal section of the interior valleys of California.

Clue Word _ _ _ _ _ _ _ _ _

Puzzle # 16

_____ Dogribs, the Crees, Tananas, and the other tribes lived and thrived in the Subarctic in the dense forests of interior Canada and Alaska, and the treeless region north of the forests was home to these tribes.

H		C			E	Y		
			H	W			I	A
I	A			C		N		
	E			P	H			
Y		P				E		N
			C	E			A	
	P	A		I			Y	C
C			H	N				
		H	W			A		P

Clue Word _ _ _ _ _ _ _ _ _

Puzzle # 17

_____ ___Aleuts lived in the region of North America as well as Greenland.

M					N			
I	N	D	S					
K	E	S			A	D		N
	A		E	N				
		K	O		D	N		
			S	I		M		
O		E	A			I	N	D
					K	S	O	A
			D					K

Clue Word _ _ _ _ _ _ _ _ _

Puzzle # 18

The first _____ to explore America were probably the daring people known as the Vikings or Norsemen during the 9th or 10th century.

	N		E					P
A			P	N	S	E		O
		O	A				S	
		E		P				N
S		P	O		N			A
N				S		U		
	S				P	R		
E		R	N	E	O	O		S
O					R		U	

Clue Word _ _ _ _ _ _ _ _ _

Puzzle # 19   *Note: Two "E's" in this word

	R			9	4		1	3
		1	W		3			N
	3	4	1					
	A					1	D	
N		D		W		4		R
	W	R					N	
					D	W	R	
R			4			A		
I	D		9	R			3	

After the pope divided the world into "Two parts," the so-called "Line of Demarcation" was _____ ____, ran from the North Pole to the South Pole through a point about 300 miles west of the Azores.

Clue Word _ _ _ _ _ _ _ _ _

Puzzle # 20

	E		R	O	U			C
T		C		E		O		
		U	T		C			
R	A		C		Q			O
		T				C		
E			A		R		Q	I
			I		T	Q		
				Q		U		R
O			U	R	E		C	

Spanish colonies in America quickly realized in 1522 that the "New World" (America) offered them an opportunity __ _____ land, wealth, and power.

Clue Word _ _ _ _ _ _ _ _ _

Puzzle # 21

A _____ ___ and major contribution of Spain was the introduction of Christianity into the New World. The Spanish abolished the practice of human sacrifice and converted millions of Indians to Roman Catholicism, thereby incorporating the Spanish language into America, even to the present day.

C			F		G			
L	R		C		A	Y		
	G	A		R		O		
O			R	A		E		
	F		Y		O		R	
		C		F	E			O
		O		C		F	E	
		Y	O		R		C	G
		G		E				Y

Clue Word _ _ _ _ _ _ _ _ _

Puzzle # 22

Robert Cavelier de La Salle, of France and Quebec, traveled to the Great Lakes and the Ohio River valley. Sailing down the Mississippi River to the Gulf of Mexico, when a _____ _____ of what he named "Louisiana" in honor of the French King Louis XIV.

	1			I	M		A	
	6				8	L	M	I
	2	I			L			8
		6	8		1	I		
1				M				L
		M	6		C	1		
I			M			6		
A	C	1	L				I	
	M		I	1			8	

Clue Word _ _ _ _ _ _ _ _ _

Puzzle # 23

N		I		H	E			
		O	G		I			
E	S	H						I
	L		F		H			
		E		O		L		
			I		L		S	
O						N	I	L
			H		O	E		
			L	S		F		N

Clue Word _ _ _ _ _ _ _ _ _

Like other nations along the Atlantic coast of Europe, _____ __ England wanted its share of trade with the East. In 1497 and again in 1498, King Henry VII sent the Italian navigator John Cabot to search for a Northwest Passage to the Orient. Cabot sailed along the east coast of North America from Newfoundland to Chesapeake Bay and claimed the region for England.

Puzzle # 24

		H	G		N	R	D	E
			E					
N			I		R	U		T
	I	G	E	R		T		
		D				I		
		T		D	I	E	R	
T		N	R		D			I
				I				
E	R	I	H		G	D		

_____ ____ reign of Queen Elizabeth I, the granddaughter of King Henry VII, England grew stronger and more adventurous. In the 1560s and 1570s, daring English sailors called "Sea Dogs" began to challenge Spanish control of the seas. Some Sea Dogs, such as Sir John Hawkins, smuggled slaves and English goods into Spanish America. Others, like Sir Francis Drake, preyed on Spanish treasure ships.

Clue Word _ _ _ _ _ _ _ _ _

Puzzle # 25

The English attacks on ships and colonies angered ___ ____ __ Spain, King Philip II. In the summer of 1588, he sent the "Spanish Armada", a mighty fleet of 130 ships, to conquer England. The Spanish Armada was met by a force of smaller vessels sailed by the English. Although the English ships were no match for the Spanish Armada in size and firepower, they were swift and easy to handle. The English skillfully outmaneuvered these attackers and prevented the Armada from landing any of its troops.

I	K	O		F		N		G
	E				O			
		N				F	O	
	F				G	K		E
K	O		N		E		I	F
E		H	T				N	
	H	K				E		
			E				K	
G		E		T		H	F	I

Clue Word _ _ _ _ _ _ _ _ _

Puzzle # 26

In the search for a Northwest Passage, the English mariner, Sir Martin _____ sailed in 1576, reached Baffin Island, and explored _____ Bay.

			F	R		S		
F		O						
R	I		O		H		F	
	I	B	H		E			
O								S
	R		R	I	O			
	O		H		S		E	R
						I		B
	B		I	R				

Clue Word _ _ _ _ _ _ _ _ _

Puzzle # 27

The first permanent English settlement in America was established at _____ in the region called Virginia.

				O	M		A
	W		M		S		
	T	A					W
S			O		T		M
	J		N			A	
M	E		W				S
E				M		O	
	S		J		E		
T	O	N					

Clue Word _ _ _ _ _ _ _ _ _

Puzzle # 28

Y					M	L		
P							Y	T
H	O		S					
M	Y	T		P				
			L		S			
				T		P	U	H
					T		O	S
T	M							P
		P	H					Y

_____ landing was the second permanent English colony in North America, located at _____, Massachusetts, near Cape Cod (earlier, John Smith had named this region New England).

Clue Word _ _ _ _ _ _ _ _ _

Puzzle # 29

A ship named and sailed by the Separatists whom lived in the Netherlands and sailed the _____, to Massachusetts in September of 1620.

			Y				E	O
		O		R	E			
F		R	O					L
	A			F	R			
	M	L				Y	F	
			A	Y			M	
A					M	E		Y
		E	O		F			
E	O				A			

Clue Word _ _ _ _ _ _ _ _ _

Puzzle # 30

__ _____ colonists whom were attacked more and more as newcomers, kept the customs they had known in England. As the years went by, however, the colonists began to create a distinctly American culture.

	H				I			G
			L			O		T
		O		S		H		
	O					T	G	H
		I		N				
L	S	G					N	
		E		L		G		
		H			G			
S			T				L	

Clue Word _ _ _ _ _ _ _ _ _

Puzzle # 31

A major immigrant group in colonial America consisted __ _____, which migrated from England and were Africans captured and enslaved in the mid-1700s. They and their descendants constituted about 20 percent of the population of the English colonies.

E		S	R					V
			A				E	Y
	A	V						
R	E			Y				
			A		E			
				O			V	S
					R	O		
L	S				O			
Y					F	A		E

Clue Word _ _ _ _ _ _ _ _ _

Puzzle # 32

B				K				T
	L	S					K	
					H	C		L
	A	L	H					
	T		A		L		H	
				E	L	C		
T		E	S					
	S					B	T	
A				T				E

The slave trade brought thousands of captives from Europe to America, enriching many "first families" of colonial times, such as the Byrds of Virginia and the Livingstons of New York. Due to harsh conditions on the slave ships, many of ___ _____ that were Africans died en route to America.

Clue Word _ _ _ _ _ _ _ _ _

Puzzle # 33

About nine-tenths of the colonists made their living __ _____. Although farms varied in size and type, most of them were small, family-operated, and self-supporting.

	N		R				A	
		F	A	G				I
		A	Y		F		N	
		M						
G				I				F
					N			
	R		F		M	B		
Y				A	R	G		
	I				B		F	

Clue Word _ _ _ _ _ _ _ _ _

Puzzle # 34

_____ __ _ industry in every well-established community was because local industries served colonists' need. Blacksmiths shod horses and produced tools and ironware. Coopers made Barrels, leatherworkers turned out shoes, and animal harnesses. Cabinet makers built furniture. Millers operated gristmills to grind grain into flour.

		H	W	G				
							T	
	R	O		H		I		
O		N	H					I
G			I		T			W
W					O	T		A
		I		W		R	A	
	G							
				I	R	W		

Clue Word _ _ _ _ _ _ _ _ _

Puzzle # 35

C								R
				A	T	E		
A		R		S			H	
	C		A	T		E		
R		H				A		T
		A		C	H		M	
	S			M		N		A
	R	T	C					
H								M

Clue Word _ _ _ _ _ _ _ _ _

_____ from New England carried on lousy trade & commerce, which were regulated in accordance with England's mercantilist policies. The American colonies exported raw materials to England and imported finished products mainly from that country.

Puzzle # 36

	R					S		
		H	F			S		
	H		I			U		O
H	F			T				R
S			F		R			H
A				U			S	F
F		O			U		A	
		A		O	S			
						T		

___ _____ established as religion was officially supported for the church by taxes. Anglicanism (The Episcopal Church) was the official religion of Virginia, Maryland, Georgia, the Carolinas, and New York. Puritanism (which came to be called Congregationalism) was established in Massachusetts, Connecticut, and New Hampshire.

Clue Word _ _ _ _ _ _ _ _ _

Puzzle # 37

The growth of tolerance in America was rooted by the complexity of various immigrating Europeans from various countries such as the Dutch, Germans, and others. The varying populations worshiping included Jews, Catholics, Baptists, and Christians. Lutherans and Presbyterians, in the 1700s, and because of this America _____ without the lack of tolerance.

			O		E		I	H
P	E	W						
I			D		W		S	
	R	D		W				
W		S				R		D
				E		H	W	
	S		E		I			W
						S	H	P
R	W		S					

Clue Word _ _ _ _ _ _ _ _ _

Puzzle # 38

"_____" ___ the Great Awakening, religious enthusiasm tended to weaken many colonists; this trend was reversed in the 1730s and 1740s. A new religion or religious movement, The Great Awakening, attracted many followers. Traveling clergymen preached fiery sermons that stirred up crowds, promising salvation for the repentant and eternal punishment for the wicked. The Great Awakening stimulated church building, the founding of new sects, and the growth of a spirit of concern for the poor and oppressed.

K	B					N		
	A				P			
W			M		E	I	P	
T			E	C				
		A						O
				N	A			S
			C		M			
B	T		A				S	M
		E						I

Clue Word _ _ _ _ _ _ _ _ _

Puzzle # 39

The earliest English colonies were of two types: controlled either by trading _____ or by individual proprietors. In the 1620s, a third type emerged.

A						N		
C	I				P			
			M		E	I	P	
O			E	C				
E								O
				N	A			S
	O	N	C		M			
			A				S	M
		M						I

Clue Word _ _ _ _ _ _ _ _ _

Puzzle # 40

	L	W		D	S			H
D								O
		E	H		L			
E	D	S						
		N				W		
					D	T	E
			D		W	L		
S								N
T			S	E		H	D	

_____ local town meetings represented a special form of local government in New England. People in this region settled close to one another in small villages. The center of village political activity was the Town Hall, where town meetings were held. In open discussions, the colonists passed laws, levied taxes to support ministers and local schools, and selected local officials and representatives to the colonial legislature. The town meeting was (and is) a good example of direct democracy.

Clue Word _ _ _ _ _ _ _ _ _

Puzzle # 41

___ _____ formed special militia forces for each colony, comprised of local groups of armed citizens. Due to slow communications and travel in colonial times, colonists could not rely on the help of regular English troops in emergencies. If an Indian attack or other disorder occurred, "militiamen" were ready to spring into action together to protect the community.

		L	C				L
	A		A				S
	H		L		L		T
				L		T	H
		L				O	
A		C		S			
O			S		L		
C				H		L	
E					O	L	H

Clue Word _ _ _ _ _ _ _ _

*Note: Two "L's" in this puzzle

Puzzle # 42

_____ facilities in the colonies were quite limited. Wealthy families had tutors for their children or sent them to private academies or schools in England. In most towns and cities, schooling of some sort was available to local residents. However, in remote areas, there were no schools at all, and in most colonies, it was forbidden to teach slave children to read or write.

I	E	N						
			A	C				
		A	N			D		O
E	A		O					
	N			U			D	
					D		N	T
U					C	A		
				I	N			
						C	U	D

Clue Word _ _ _ _ _ _ _ _ _

Puzzle # 43

B	E	T		J	O			
				S			E	
					T	U	E	
		O		U		C		U
E			T		C			
T		U		E		B		
	O	C						
	T		B		U	U		
			O				S	T

Clue Word _ _ _ _ _ _ _ _ _

Subjects taught to most schoolchildren were not advanceable beyond the three R's (reading, 'riting, 'rithmetic). Pupils often learned using a _____ or related to a New England primer using a hornbook. The hornbook was a sheet of paper mounted on a board and protected with a thin covering of transparent animal horn. It displayed the alphabet, the Lord's Prayer, and Roman numerals.

Puzzle # 44

G	E						I	
T					N			R
I		O		R	R	E		
			N	G		R		
	T		E		I			
	G		R	P				
	E	R	T					I
P			I					R
	I						P	T

_____ via the Boston Newsletter, started in 1704, and was the first colonial newspaper to last more than a short time. By the middle of the century, weekly newspapers were being published in almost every colony. At a time when communication was limited, newspapers did much to shape American public opinion.

Clue Word _ _ _ _ _ _ _ _ _

*Note: Two "R's" in this Puzzle

Puzzle # 45

Libraries during the colonial period were available, but time for _____ books or reading wasn't readily available to most people. Moreover, not everyone knew how to read. Books imported from Europe were expensive and primarily purchased by ministers, lawyers, and wealthy merchants. The only books in most homes were the Bible and an almanac. Over time, leisure and literacy increased. The first circulating library was founded in Philadelphia in 1731.

	S		I					
		Y	U				G		S
		T		N	Y				U
Y							A	S	
		S					I		
	D	I						Y
U				I	Y		N	
N		D			G	S		
					U		A	

Clue Word _ _ _ _ _ _ _ _ _

Puzzle # 46

A _____ ____ and or the earliest settlers' homes and shelters were primarily of two types: either bark-covered huts or log cabins. Later, when more attention could be paid to comfort and beauty, colonists built better homes. In New England, the typical colonial house was a low, wood cottage with a sloping roof, simple and with little outside decoration (known as the "saltbox" style). In New York, the Dutch influence was evident in brick houses with steeply slanted roofs. Many homes in Pennsylvania were built and made of local stone.

E		O	T				B
				H		U	
	U		I			T	
	O			E		B	T
	T		H		M		
B	E			O		H	
	M			B		E	
	H	L					
I					L	L	O

Clue Word _ _ _ _ _ _ _ _ _

Puzzle # 47

O					A	N		R
V	N	A					U	
				O	N			
	A	N					H	
			N	H	O			
	G					V	E	
			G	U				
	V					G	A	E
N		G	R					U

Clue Word _ _ _ _ _ _ _ _ _

Colonial food was plentiful but plain. Women did most of the cooking in iron pots ____ ____ _ fire in the fireplace. The meat was roasted on rotating spits, and bread and cakes were baked in ovens built into the fireplace. There was no refrigeration, and the meat was salted, dried, or smoked. Vegetables and fruits were pickled, dried, or preserved.

Puzzle # 48

B		A			S	
				O	K	T
	U			K		
	T	K	O		A	S
	R			B		
K	O		S		A	T
		E			B	
U	K	E				
	T			S		R

Clue Word _ _ _ _ _ _ _ _

___ _____ of war began in 1753 when the French started to build a chain of forts from Lake Erie south to the Ohio River. Governor Robert Dinwiddie of Virginia then sent George Washington, a 21-year-old surveyor, and fellow Virginian into the area. His mission was to warn the French that they were trespassing on English territory and to demand that they leave. The French rejected the demand and continued to strengthen their position in the Ohio Valley.

Puzzle # 49

___ ____ ___ French built Fort Duquesne at the point where the Allegheny and Monongahela rivers joined to form the Ohio River. This strategic site (present-day Pittsburgh) was key to the Ohio Valley and a main gateway to the West. This time, Dinwiddie sent a force of militiamen men led by George Washington to take Fort Duquesne. About 40 miles from the fort, the colonial forces defeated a small group of French soldiers and quickly built an outpost called "Fort Necessity." However, French soldiers returned with reinforcements and drove out the Virginians. This encounter marked the beginning of the French and Indian War.

				T		4	H
T	1	I	7				
		N			T	I	
	7					N	5
4				E			7
5	E				4		
	7	1			5		
					1	N	7	E
E	N		T				

Clue Word _ _ _ _ _ _ _ _ _

Puzzle # 50

The _____ _____ of Union was a British initiative to organize the colonies against the French. In 1754, representatives from seven colonies met in Albany, New York. The Albany Congress had two main purposes: (1) to gain the help of the Iroquois Confederacy and (2) to unite the colonies for defense purposes. To achieve these aims, Benjamin Franklin of Pennsylvania proposed the Albany Plan of Union, which would have created a congress of delegates representing all colonies. This "grand council" would have the power to maintain an army, levy taxes, deal with the Indians, and control westward expansion.

		N			Y			
	Y		L					T
			A				H	N
Y		E		A				
	L	H		N		A	T	
				A		N		Y
L	B				H			
H					A		N	
			T			L		

Clue Word _ _ _ _ _ _ _ _ _

Puzzle # 51   *Note: Two "A's" in this puzzle

	N	E						
T					L	N	O	
				P	H		E	
N		P		O				H
			A		N			
L				H		T		F
	H		E	A				
	A	L	H					O
					H	A		

Both Britain and the colonial legislatures rejected Franklin's plan. Britain felt that a union of colonies would make them too strong. The failure __ ____ ____was indicative of the individual colonies' reluctance to give up any of their powers to a "Grand Council." Despite its defeat, the Albany Plan indicated that at least some colonists were considering union.

Clue Word _ _ _ _ _ _ _ _ _

Puzzle # 52

H		D						E
		Y	O	L				
		E	H				W	U
			T					O
	W					H		
Y					L			
L	Y				H	W		
				O	T	L		
						E		Y

Even before the French and Indian War ended, the colonists demonstrated that ____ _____ oppose stricter British control of trade. In 1761, officials began to use writs of assistance to stop colonial merchants from illegally trading with foreign nations. The writs were general search warrants that allowed customs officers to enter any ship, home, or warehouse and search for smuggled goods.

Clue Word _ _ _ _ _ _ _ _ _

Puzzle # 53

In 1763, the British _____ an action that irritated the Americans concerning the Ohio Valley. After the French were defeated, colonists began to pour into this desirable region. The Indians there became alarmed. In the spring of 1763, they rose under the leader named "Pontiac." The Indians destroyed most of the British frontier forts in the area and killed many white settlers. Before Pontiac's Rebellion was put down in the fall, to avoid further trouble, Britain issued the Proclamation of 1763.

	M				C	P		
A	R		L	I				
		A	A			I		L
		M	I					C
				A		O		
I					O	L		
M		C			R			
				O	A		S	P
		S	C				L	

Clue Word _ _ _ _ _ _ _ _ _

Puzzle # 54

The British Proclamation of 1763 was __ _____ that; (1) ordered all settlers in the Ohio Valley to move back east, (2) forbade the establishment of new settlements west of the Appalachians, and (3) prohibited traders from entering the region without government approval.

			L				D	N
	L	E					I	
		D		O	I			
L							T	C
C			T	E	D			L
E	I							D
			I	U		L		
	T						N	U
I	E				T			

Clue Word _ _ _ _ _ _ _ _ _

Puzzle # 55

		C	O		6		T	
7		6			T			
						C	7	
		1						F
	A		4		7		6	
F						T		
	C	O						
			6			F		4
	T		C		1	6		

Clue Word _ _ _ _ _ _ _ _ _

The ___ __ ____ was designed by the British to raise more money from the American colonies. The law was the Sugar ___ __ ____. It increased duties on refined sugar, textiles, and other goods imported from non-British sources. (Duties are taxes on imports.) To discourage smuggling, the act lowered the duty on colonial imports of foreign molasses.

Puzzle # 56

6		T	5			1		
	F	5	C					
			F			6		O
	1			6				T
T				O			C	
1		O			A			
				7	F	1		
		C			1	7		A

Clue Word _ _ _ _ _ _ _ _ _

Another source of colonial irritation was the Quartering ___ __ ____. This British law was passed in response to a request by Thomas Gage, commander of British forces in America. The act required colonial legislatures to provide funds, living quarters, and supplies to help meet the cost of keeping British troops in America.

Puzzle # 57

No other British law of the 1760s stirred up such a storm of protest as the "Stamp Act of 1765." It taxed newspapers, almanacs, pamphlets, playing cards, and legal _____ (wills, licenses, deeds, and so on). A government stamp had to be placed on each of these articles to show that the tax had been paid.

					N	T			D
T	U							
					D	T	E	
				M	S		C	
E		O				S		T
	S		N	T				
	M	S	C					
							O	N
D			U	E				

Clue Word _ _ _ _ _ _ _ _ _

Puzzle # 58

What was known as the "Boston Massacre" occurred in 1770 in Boston, when _____ between the colonists and British troops were tense. One March evening, a crowd of Bostonians shouted insults and threw snowballs at British soldiers. The soldiers fired into the crowd, killing five people and wounding six others. Angry citizens called the event "The Boston Massacre."

	S		E		L			
T	L			O		E		
	R					A	L	
		O		E			A	
A			I		S			T
	T			A		N		
	O	S					R	
		R		N			T	E
			L		R			

Clue Word _ _ _ _ _ _ _ _ _

Puzzle # 59

F		C				4	
	A				1		C
		1		7	T		
T	F						
			O	C	4		
						A	O
			A	F		1	
O			7			T	
	1					7	7

Clue Word _ _ _ _ _ _ _ _

*Note: Two "7's" in this answer and puzzle

Anger and opposition erupted once again when Parliament passed the "Tea ____" __ ____. This law was designed to aid the financially troubled British East India Company. The Tea Act allowed the company to ship tea directly to America without paying the heavy duty required in England. A small import tax still had to be paid in America, but the company could easily undersell colonial importers of English tea as well as smugglers of foreign tea.

Puzzle # 60

Determined to make the colonies respect its authority, the British government moved _____ __ punish Massachusetts for the Boston Tea Party. In 1774, Parliament passed the four "Coercive Acts."

L				T			U
		C		Y		O	
	Y				L	I	
		Q					
Y		Q			U		C
			U	K			
	O	L			C		
	Y		I		L		
T			K			L	

Clue Word _ _ _ _ _ _ _ _ _

Puzzle # 61

The Coercive ___ __ ____ were: (1) The port of Boston was closed until the colonists paid for the destroyed tea. (2) The people were deprived of the right to elect certain officials, select judges, and hold town meetings. (3) British soldiers accused of crimes in Massachusetts were to be tried in England, not in the colony. (4) People in all colonies were required to feed and house British soldiers.

			1				
	T						4
7			O	4	A	T	
T	4	F	A			7	
		7	4	C	O		
		O			4	7	A
		7	C	F	1		T
O						F	
					T	A	

Clue Word _ _ _ _ _ _ _ _ _

Puzzle # 62   *Note: Two "7's" in this puzzle

A _____ ____ taken by the First Continental Congress held in September of 1774 was; (1) issuing a Declaration of Rights, (2) to not trade with Britain until the Coercive Acts were repealed, and to refuse "English Goods." The declaration also called the Coercive Acts unconstitutional and asked "the people" not to obey these laws.

		O	E					
				O	M		S	
	R	E	S			T		
P			J	S		M	R	
E								J
	J	S		M	R			P
		A			S	P	J	
	S		M	E				
					J	R		

Clue Word _ _ _ _ _ _ _ _ _

Puzzle # 63

	N		7	A			8	
A	8	T				7		
1			N			3		
O					D			
		8	A		N	O		
			O					A
		D			1			O
		N					D	1
	1			7	O		3	

About six months after the Continental Congress adjourned, war broke out between the American colonies and England. The conflict was named the "Revolutionary War." It was to last from 1775 __ ____ ___ result in American independence. But independence was not the colonists' goal at first and never the goal for "some of them."

Clue Word _ _ _ _ _ _ _ _ _

Puzzle # 64

In defense of Thomas Gage, the British governor, the Massachusetts assembly met secretly and prepared for war. ____ _____ about these preparations, however, in April 1775, he sent a detachment of soldiers from Boston to Lexington to capture the "rebel" ringleaders John Hancock and Samuel Adams. However, the colonists learned of Gage's plan in advance. On the night of April 18, 1775, Paul Revere and another patriot, William Dawes, rode through the countryside, spreading news of the oncoming British.

	N						E	
	D			E	U			
					D	O		F
G					O			A
		E	D		A	N		
N			E					G
D		G	O					
			A	D			O	
	F						U	

Clue Word _ _ _ _ _ _ _ _

*Note: Two "G's" in this puzzle

Puzzle # 65

Three weeks after _____ and Concord, in May 1775, the Second Continental Congress assembled in Philadelphia at the State House (later called Independence Hall). John Hancock of Massachusetts was elected president. The delegates faced the choice of giving in to the home country or continuing to resist by force if necessary.

E			N	X			O	
		I	E					L
X	T					E		
	E			N	X	L		
		I		T				E
	N	L	E			X		
	X						N	I
N					N	G		
			I	G				T

Clue Word _ _ _ _ _ _ _ _

*Note: Two "N's" in this puzzle

Puzzle # 66

Years before the war started, Ethan Allen had _____ a militia in the region of Vermont. Allen's men called themselves the "Green Mountain Boys." In May 1775, as the Second Continental Congress was meeting, a small force of Allen's militia secretly crossed Lake Champlain and attacked the British forts at Ticonderoga and Crown Point in northeastern New York. The Americans captured the forts, seized badly needed cannon and ammunition, and sent these supplies to aid the Americans in the Boston area.

	O					A		Z
	N		A			O	E	
				E	R			
E		G					O	
I			G		E			N
	D					G		E
			D	O				
	E	A			I		Z	
O		N					A	

Clue Word _ _ _ _ _ _ _ _ _

Puzzle # 67

C			R			O		
			C					U
G	E					Y	C	
R		A		U				
	U			O			G	
				G		U		C
	R	B					U	
O					U			
		Y			B			A

Clue Word _ _ _ _ _ _ _ _ _

To obtain a commanding position over Boston and its harbor, __ _____ the Americans secretly occupied Breed's Hill near Bunker Hill and began to fortify it. On June 17, the British attacked the Americans. The 'Redcoats' were pushed back with heavy losses in their first two attempts. But they captured the hill in their third charge when the colonists' supply of ammunition ran out. In this Battle of 'Bunker Hill' (actually fought on Breed's Hill), the Americans inflicted far more casualties than they suffered.

Puzzle # 68

	L				N			
			L	C		E		
		E	I				H	K
I	U			H				
T								E
				C			U	T
U	H				L	C		
	I		H	U				
		K				L		

Americans had better ____ __ ___ South. Early in 1776, militiamen crushed a 1500-man loyalist force at Moore's Creek Bridge, in North Carolina. Later that year, the British tried to attack Charleston, South Carolina, but they were driven off by American troops.

Clue Word _ _ _ _ _ _ _ _ _

Puzzle # 69

More and more Americans began to feel that the colonies had to break away from England. "The spirit of independence" was sparked by a pamphlet called "Common Sense," _____ in January 1776 by Thomas Paine, a recent immigrant from England. Paine blamed the king for the colonists' troubles. He argued that it was foolish for an entire continent to be controlled by a small island 3000 miles away. In stirring words, Paine called upon America to "break its ties" with Britain.

	S	D	H	B				
						S	E	P
			E		U	D		
	U	P		D				
H				L				E
			H		I	P		
		L		H				
P	I							
					I	U	D	

Clue Word _ _ _ _ _ _ _ _ _

Puzzle # 70

In June 1776, Richard Henry Lee of Virginia introduced a resolution in Congress _____ that these united colonies are, and of right ought to be, free and independent states. Congress then chose a committee to draw up a "Declaration of Independence," which was written by Thomas Jefferson.

	L				D			N
	N		L	A				
		C			R	I		G
C	I					D	E	
				I				
	A	N					I	C
L		A	E			G		
				L	G		C	
D			R				N	

Clue Word _ _ _ _ _ _ _ _ _

Puzzle # 71

				T			N
				D	G		E
O	D	N					
N	E			O		G	
		N		G		E	
	G		L			T	D
					T	L	A
G		D	T				
L			N				

Clue Word _ _ _ _ _ _ _ _

*Note: Two "N's" in this puzzle

After the British left Boston in the spring of 1776, the war shifted from New _____ __ the middle colonies. In the two years that followed, both sides won important victories.

Puzzle # 72

S	R			Y			
Y					M		R
		H		T		U	
	H	Y	A		S		
	U					M	
	S		H	M	T		
	S		M		H		
M		R					H
							M

Recognizing the strategic value of New York City, Washington moved his ____ _____ to defend the area. At the same time, have made plans to capture it. In July 1776, supported by a strong fleet, the British occupied Staten Island. During the next four months, they drove the Continental Army out of Brooklyn Heights on Long Island, Eastern Heights in Manhattan, and White Plains in Westchester County. Washington's skills in handling the army kept it from being completely destroyed by the more powerful army.

Clue Word _ _ _ _ _ _ _ _

Puzzle # 73

_____ _____ famous American spy, Nathan Hale before his execution said, "I only regret that I have but one life to lose for my country."

P		A	E					O
		D		N				U
			U			D	E	
		U					T	
	E		P		H		A	
	A				E			
	T	H			N			
D				P		H		
					T	U		N

Clue Word _ _ _ _ _ _ _ _

Puzzle # 74

Instead of proceeding up the Hudson, Howe sailed from New York City to Chesapeake Bay. He then _____ __ the American capital, Philadelphia. Washington tried to stop the British but was defeated at Brandywine on September 11, 1777. Howe occupied Philadelphia later that month. When the Americans attempted to drive him out, they were repelled at Germantown. Washington then withdrew and set up winter quarters at nearby Valley Forge. That winter (1777-1778) was a bitter one for the American army.

	D				E	O		M
				R				
H	R		O					E
		R		C			H	
		H				M		
	N			M		D		
E					M		A	H
			A					
M		C	R				O	

Clue Word _ _ _ _ _ _ _ _ _

Puzzle # 75

			G			U	N	
			Q	R	I			
I	G					Q		
		O		C			Q	T
Q			U		T			N
T	N				O			
		I					R	G
			I		G			
	M	T			U			

Clue Word _ _ _ _ _ _ _ _ _

" _____ " __ Thomas Paine, 1776: "These are the times that try men's souls. The summer soldier and the sunshine patriot will, in this crisis, shrink from the service of their country; but he that stands by it now, deserves the love and thanks of man and woman."

Puzzle # 76

Hoping to weaken England, other European powers—France, Spain, and the Netherlands—had been secretly helping the Americans with supplies, weapons, ___ _____ ever since 1776. After Saratoga, which demonstrated that American victory was possible, France agreed to enter into an open alliance with the United States. Benjamin Franklin, a congressional representative in France, played a key role in the successful negotiations. Early in 1778, France and the United States signed military and trade agreements.

						I	E	
E			D		T			C
	I			R		C	T	
		R		C		D		
	N	T		E			R	
D			A		D			N
	C	D						
				D				

Clue Word _ _ _ _ _ _ _ _ _

*Note: Two "D's" in this puzzle

Puzzle # 77

Fighting also occurred on the Western Frontier in a region called the Northwest Territory. Here, the British were stirring up the Indians to attack American settlements. To end these raids, George Rogers Clark led a band of frontier fighters into the area in the summer of 1778. He captured the British forts at Kaskaskia and Cahokia (in present-day Illinois) and at Vincennes (___ __ ___ Indiana). However, British reinforcements from Detroit retook Vincennes in December.

	S			N				O
		T		W				W
	I	H	W					S
			H			T		
	N	W				H	I	
		S			N			
S					I	N	A	
H				O		W		
A				H			O	

Puzzle # 78

Clue Word _ _ _ _ _ _ _ _ _

*Note: Two "W's" in this puzzle

Before the French fleet came to aid the Continentals, American sea power was very limited. There were a few small warships and _ _____ __ privateers. (Privateers are privately owned merchant vessels and fishing boats fitted with guns and are authorized to attack enemy ships. These naval units transported supplies and munitions from Europe and seized military equipment en route to British forces fighting in America.

	U	R	N					B
		N	R				F	
E			U	B				
U							E	O
	N			F			U	
O	F							R
				M	B			U
	O				U	B		
B					N	A	R	

Clue Word _ _ _ _ _ _ _ _ _

Puzzle # 79

		E		P	L		N	
		J				E	S	
P		N	U					
	O		E					
N				O				S
				A		U		
				J	P			U
	L	P			S			
	J		N	L		A		

Clue Word _ _ _ _ _ _ _ _ _

An outstanding American hero was John ____ _____. This Scottish-born sea captain seized many British merchant ships and raided the coast of England warship 'Serapis' on September 23, 1779. In the most dramatic naval battle of the Revolution, Jones forced the 'Serapis' to surrender and sailed back to America. Another war hero, John Barry, a native of Ireland, won fame for his skill in capturing British fighting ships.

Puzzle # 80

Puzzle # 81

G		F		U				
					U	T	F	
		O		N				M
U	M						N	
		H	G	F				
	F						O	G
N			A		G			
A	U	T						
				T		N		A

Benedict Arnold, the ___ _____ really valiantly on behalf of the American cause in the early part of the war. He also played an important role in the Continental victory at Saratoga, in 1780. He was given command of West Point, a fort controlling the Hudson River. Soon afterward, he entered into a plot to surrender West Point to the British. Arnold's plan was discovered when John André, an English officer with whom Arnold was negotiating, was captured with plans of the fort in his possession. The name, Benedict Arnold, became synonymous with 'traitor'.

Clue Word _ _ _ _ _ _ _ _ _

Failing to make headway in New England and the middle colonies, the British turned their attention to the South. They captured Savannah in December 1778 and Charleston __ ___ ____. In August of that year, British forces defeated an American army under Gates at Camden, South Carolina. However, a British attempt to invade North Carolina was beaten back when sharp-shooting frontiersmen defeated a Loyalist force at King's Mountain in October.

Puzzle # 82								
								I
1			8	Y	O			
8	N	A						
	8	M			7		1	
			A		Y			
	Y		O			A	M	
						I	N	1
		Y	A	8				O
7								

Clue Word _ _ _ _ _ _ _ _ _

A notable American of the Revolutionary Era was William Billings (1746-1800), the first important American composer. He was a Boston tuner with __ _____ training. But his enthusiasm and inventiveness inspired him to write hundreds of lively and charming hymn tunes, which were eagerly performed by the church choirs of his day. He was an ardent patriot, and his song "Chester" was a favorite among both civilians and continental troops.

			N			O		
N			S		O		M	
	L	S						
L	A	C						
			O		U			
						M	I	A
						I	N	
	C		U		A			O
		U			S			

Clue Word _ _ _ _ _ _ _ _ _

Puzzle # 83

	8				2			
O		N			R			
			N	I				O
					F	2	8	
I	N					O	7	
7	2	F						
2			7	I				
			O			I		1
		O				8		

Clue Word _ _ _ _ _ _ _ _ _

Although the British still occupied New York City and the Southern seaports, their hopes for victory were shattered. The English public was tired of the war and sought peace ___ __ ____, Parliament voted to end hostilities and began peace talks. In the "Treaty of Paris", signed in September 1783, Britain acknowledged the independence of 13 colonies. The boundaries of the new nation were set as the Atlantic Ocean on the east, the Mississippi River on the west, Canada on the north, and Florida on the south. Britain granted Americans full fishing rights and returned Florida to Spain.

Puzzle # 84

U			G	R				
			E				G	T
	T		T			E		
				E		T		
E		H				D		N
		U		H				
		R			D		U	
G	T				E			
				T	R			H

A notable American of the Revolutionary Era was Paul Cliffe (1759-1817). He was the first Black American to become wealthy, starting out as a seaman and gradually acquiring his own fleet of ships. _____ ____ Revolutionary War, he and his brother went to court in their native Massachusetts. They argued that denied the vote, they were suffering from the same taxation without representation that agitated white patriots.

Clue Word _ _ _ _ _ _ _ _ _

Puzzle # 85

The newly independent United States faced _ _____ ___ difficulties. One of the most troubling issues was the creation of an acceptable form of government. The first type of government the Americans set up proved unsatisfactory and had to be abandoned. The second one was far more effective. Not only did it meet the needs of the times, but it has also survived to the present day.

U	O		N					
							F	A
A			O		E			
N		M		U		R		
		R		M		U		B
			E		F			U
O	F							
					U		V	N

Clue Word _ _ _ _ _ _ _ _ _

Puzzle # 86

During the Revolution, the Continental Congress drafted 2 written constitutions, called the "Articles of Confederation," ___ __ ____, the Articles provided a central government for the new nation for eight years—a time often called the Confederation period. The Articles of Confederation gave Congress a limited number of powers for governing the nation. All other powers and functions of government were exercised by the separate states. As a result, the central government was unable to deal effectively with many problems it faced.

	O							7
				N			O	I
			2		R			8
		R					7	
		O	7		N	2		
	N					1		
O			I		F			
2	1			8				
R							I	

Clue Word _ _ _ _ _ _ _ _ _

Puzzle # 87

T		O	Y					
C				D	L			
					H	E		
Y	O	C						
		U	T		D	O		
						E	U	Y
	L	T						
			O	E				D
					T	Y		U

Clue Word _ _ _ _ _ _ _ _ _

"In the new code of Laws, which I suppose it will be necessary for you to make, I desire you would remember the ladies and be more generous and favorable to them than your ancestors. Do not put such unlimited power into the hands of the husbands. Remember, all men would be tyrants if ____ ____." - Abigail Adams in a letter to her husband, John Adams, written in 1776 when the Second Continental Congress began drafting the Articles of Confederation.

Puzzle # 88

American History Sudoku Trivia

Many Americans liked the weak type of government set up by the Articles. After all, they had just fought a revolution to be rid of strong central authority (the British King and Parliament). But other Americans, especially merchants and property owners, wanted a stronger national government. People with this view began to hold meetings and work for change. In 1785, delegates from Maryland and Virginia met at Mount Vernon, Washington's home. They succeeded in settling some problems concerning shipping in the Potomac River. The success of this Mount Vernon conference prompted all states to attend the next meeting in 1786 at Annapolis, Maryland.

N				R	O			
	O		A	E	C			
A			H			F		
H							R	
		E	R	H				
	F							H
		O			C			N
		H		G			F	
		A	R					E

Clue Word _ _ _ _ _ _ _ _ _

Puzzle # 89

Only five states sent representatives to the Annapolis convention. At the urging of Alexander Hamilton of New York, however, the convention adopted a resolution requesting Congress to convene another conference the following year. The 1787 convention, held in Philadelphia's Independence Hall, would not only discuss commercial issues but also ways of improving the national government. This marked the beginning of the ___ ____ _____.

					T	P		
N			E	F			O	
		E					N	L
	H						A	N
			F	H	N			
O	L					F		
E	O				A			
	F			O	A			P
		A	P					

Clue Word _ _ _ _ _ _ _ _ _

Puzzle # 90

All the states except Rhode Island sent delegates to the Constitutional Convention. Its 55 members, often called the "Founding Fathers" or "founders," were politically experienced, realistic, and well-qualified for the task ahead. Most shared a conservative outlook. About half of them were lawyers. ____ __ ___ others were planters and merchants. Of the delegates who met in Philadelphia, the most admired was George Washington, who was elected president of the convention. Other important members included Benjamin Franklin, James Madison, and Alexander Hamilton. Absent from the convention were many outstanding revolutionary patriots.

	Y		F	H	T			
	N	F						
					A	M	Y	F
					O			E
O		T				A		N
Y			T					
T	A	M	O					
							O	N
			A	E	F		M	

Clue Word _ _ _ _ _ _ _ _ _

Puzzle # 91

	A				O			
				T		S		I
	S					O		
				E		N	T	
A			N		U			O
	Q	E		S				
		U					E	
E		T		U				
			Q				O	

Clue Word _ _ _ _ _ _ _ _ _

Constitutional compromises dealt with at the Constitutional Convention in 1787 dealt with a variety of issues, but __ _____ of how various states should be represented in the national legislature was core of them. The problem was solved by what has come to be known as "the Great Compromise." A Congress consisting of two houses was established. In the upper house, the Senate, each state would have two senators. In the lower house, the House of Representatives, each state would be represented based on population.

Puzzle # 92

The Great Compromise led to another issue: In counting the population of a state, what about slaves? The Southern States wanted the number of their representatives in the House of Representatives to be based on their total population, including slaves. However, these states did not want slaves to be counted for the purpose of direct taxation by the national government. The Northern States took the opposite position. They did not want to count slaves for representation, but they did want ___ _____ them for taxation. The difficulty was resolved by the Three-Fifths Compromise, which stated that three-fifths of the slave population would be counted for both taxation and representation.

Clue Word _ _ _ _ _ _ _ _ _

Puzzle # 93

The founders set up three branches of government: legislative, executive, and judicial. This division of governmental authority and duties is called separation of powers. The _____ _____ of the legislative branch is to make laws. The legislature, Congress, has two houses: the upper one, the Senate, consists of two members from each state, making the membership 100 since there are now 50 states. In the lower house, the House of Representatives, each state is represented according to population. The present number of members in that house is 435.

Clue Word _ _ _ _ _ _ _ _ _

Puzzle # 94

Although the delegates aimed to create a strong central government, they also wanted to ensure the states maintained adequate authority. The solution was federalism. Under a federal system, power is shared between a national government and regional governments, such as states or _____. In the United States, powers assigned to the national government are known as "delegated" powers, while those retained by the states are "reserved" powers. The Constitution also granted the national government the right to make laws that are "necessary and proper" for carrying out its delegated powers. This clause, known as the "elastic clause," allows the central government to extend its powers beyond those explicitly listed, also referred to as "implied powers."

		O			E			
I						V		E
	R		P		I		S	
				N	O		C	
		N				O		
	P		I	C				
	S		E		N		R	
P		E						C
			C			E		

Clue Word _ _ _ _ _ _ _ _ _

Puzzle # 95

E			L					
L			Y			9		8
		7				E	L	
	7			R			A	
			7		1			
	1			Y			7	
9	8	E				A		
		R						Y
								9

Clue Word _ _ _ _ _ _ _ _ _

_____ _____, it was time to elect a president to head the new government. All attention turned to George Washington, who was admired as a national hero. As head of the Army, he had shown sound judgment, courage, determination, and leadership. Americans believed that he could bring these qualities to the presidency. Washington agreed to serve, though he preferred to remain a private citizen. When the ballots of the Electoral College were counted by the first Congress in April, Washington was the unanimous choice for president. John Adams, with the second-highest number of votes, became vice president.

Puzzle # 96

O						A		T
	I	E		F	T			
		T			S			
			P			I		E
	R						T	
A		I		T				
			I			R		
			T	A		P	E	
R		O						A

Alexander Hamilton's financial program established a strong foundation for the United States. But it helped the well-to-do more than average Americans. For this reason, it aroused opposition as well as support. This division of opinion led to the nation's first political _____ ____ groups that called themselves Federalists, and Democratic-Republicans.

Clue Word _ _ _ _ _ _ _ _ _

Puzzle # 97

During Washington's eight years in office, relations with Europe were complicated by the French Revolution. This uprising, which broke out in 1789, greatly changed life and government in France. The revolution also led to a series of wars that eventually involved almost every European nation, ___ _____ affairs grew more complicated, (the wars only ended with the final defeat of Napoleon, the French emperor, in 1815.) In the conflicts between France and Britain, Americans took sides. The "Democratic-Republicans" generally favored France while Federalists usually supported Britain.

					R			E
G	F						N	
		I	N		O			F
		E		O				
	A	F				N	O	
				N		A		
A			E		S	F		
	E						S	I
S			G					

Clue Word _ _ _ _ _ _ _ _ _

Puzzle # 98

_____ ____ resulted in the French King being overthrown and executed, leading France to war with Britain, Spain, and the Netherlands. The French expected the United States to come to their aid because the two nations had signed a treaty of alliance during the American Revolution. But Washington along with Jefferson and Hamilton, felt the young nation would be harmed by joining the conflict. Washington issued a Neutrality Proclamation in April 1793, declaring the U.S. would remain neutral and warning the citizens against hostile actions towards any nation at war.

Clue Word _ _ _ _ _ _ _ _ _ _

Puzzle # 99

Clue Word _ _ _ _ _ _ _ _ _

The United States government was also having trouble with Britain. In violation of the Treaty of Paris, the British continued to occupy many forts and trading posts in the Northwest Territory. From these bases, they carried on a far-reaching fur trade. They also sold guns to the Indians and stirred up Indian attacks on American frontier settlements. Britain justified its occupation of American territory by claiming that certain provisions of the peace treaty had not been honored by the United States. (1) _____ ___ settle pre-Revolutionary debts owed by Americans to British Merchants, and (2) 'Failure' pay loyalists for property taken over by the States.

Puzzle # 100

Another sore point had to do with shipping. American foreign trade increased sharply after the _____ of war in Europe. As a neutral nation, the United States traded with both sides. To keep supplies from reaching the French, the British Navy, in 1739, began seizing neutral ships bound for France or its colonies. In less than a year, the British seized 250 U.S. Ships on many occasions, the British removed American seamen from U.S. ships and forced them to serve in the British Navy.

	O		R	A				
			U			E		
		T					R	S
	S	O			T	T		
U			O					E
		B				K	A	
B						A		
	K	A			B			
				K	U		B	

Clue Word _ _ _ _ _ _ _ _ _

Puzzle # 101

Washington sent John Jay to Britain to negotiate a settlement of differences between the two countries. A treaty signed in 1794 provided for (1) the withdrawal of British troops from the Northwest Territory. (2) _____ ___ debts owed to British creditors by Americans, and (3) compensation to American shippers for ships and cargoes seized by the British. The 'Jay Treaty' was widely criticized. This agreement between the United States and Britain succeeded in postponing a showdown with Britain until 1812.

				M				E
T		O		N	P			
	N						T	O
	M	E						
Y								A
			E			M	N	
E	P				M		O	
			N	E				Y
A				O		P		

Clue Word _ _ _ _ _ _ _ _ _

Puzzle # 102

_____ with France, already strained grew worse after the signing of the 'Jay Treaty'. As the French saw it, the Americans were ignoring their mutual aid agreement with France and moving closer to Britain. Armed French vessels began to seize American Merchant ships found for British forts. In addition, the French government refused to receive the U.S. ministers, Charles Pinckney. In 1797, Adams sent a delegation to France to try to settle the difficulties. The Americans met with three French agents who demanded payments and bribes. These demands were rejected.

	N	S			I			E
		A					I	N
I			A	T				
N	T	R						
			R	E	S			
						I	R	A
				I	R			L
S	O					R		
R			O			A	E	

Clue Word _ _ _ _ _ _ _ _ _

Puzzle # 103

		Z		T	E			Y
		E	X	A	Y		Z	D
			Z		D	H		E
	D		N	X		Y		T
X		T	Y		H	Z		N
Y		N		E	A		H	
T		D	A		X			
Z	X		E	H	N	T		
N			D	Z		X		

Clue Word _ _ _ _ _ _ _ _ _

Early the next year, American newspapers reported the demands made by the French agents, who were identified simply as X, Y, and Z. Americans were outraged by the agents' demands for a bribe, ____ ____ ____ affair as it was called, aroused a storm of anti-French protest in the United States. A popular slogan was; "Millions for defense but not one cent for tribute." In preparation for the war, congress passed a number of defense measures and then created 'The Department of the Navy'.

Puzzle # 104

At the height of the French crisis, the federalist-dominated Congress passed four harsh laws, known as the 'Alien and Sedition Acts'. (An alien is a resident non-citizen; Sedition means treason). One act raised the residence requirement for citizenship from 5 to 14 years. Another gave the president power to _____ ____ alien considered dangerous to the nation's peace and safety. The third act gave the president authority to arrest or deport enemy aliens in times of war. And fourth, made it a crime to publish "False Scandalous, and malicious writing" about the government or its officials.

Y		T	R		D			
E		D		O				Y
A		P	E		Y	D	N	R
	D	R	N					T
T		N	A		R	Y		O
O					P	R	D	
D	P	O	Y		A	N		E
N				P		O		A
			O			P		D

Clue Word _ _ _ _ _ _ _ _ _

Puzzle # 105

The United States made a better bargain with Spain, but one problem concerned navigation _____ ____ __ lower Mississippi River. A related issue involved certain privileges in New Orleans, at the mouth of the river. Americans wanted to ship goods down the Mississippi. They also wanted to deposit the goods in New Orleans and then transfer them to ocean-going vessels without paying 'duties' to Spain. This so-called 'right of deposit' was important to Western farmers because New Orleans was their outlet to Eastern and European markets.

		A	O	S	R		H	T
T			G		A	R		O
	G	O	N			I		S
N			S	O				A
		S	A		I	O		
A				N	H			I
G		N			O	T	S	
O		T	R		S			H
S	R		H	T	N	A		

Clue Word _ _ _ _ _ _ _ _ _

Puzzle # 106

A third problem concerned the disputed boundary between Georgia and Spanish Florida. Thomas Pinckney negotiated a settlement of all these issues. 'The Pinckney Treaty' was ____ ___ _____, which guaranteed Americans navigation rights on the lower Mississippi River, and the right of deposit at New Orleans. The treaty also fixed the boundary between Spanish and U.S. territories east of the Mississippi at the 31st parallel.

	W	A	N	I				7
5	I				L		1	
N	7	1				L		I
I	A		5	1		W	9	L
			W		A			
1	5	W		L	9		7	N
W		7				I	L	9
	L		7				W	1
9				W	I	7	N	

Clue Word _ _ _ _ _ _ _ _ _

Puzzle # 107

G			U	O				R
	Q		I	G		T	M	
	U	N						I
M	N		G		U		R	
Q	I					G	N	
	T		M		I		U	O
U						O	T	
	G	T		U	M		N	
N				T	Q			G

Clue Word _ _ _ _ _ _ _ _

" _____ " __. George Washington in his Farewell Address, in 1796; "It is our true policy to steer clear of permanent alliances with any portion of the foreign world"

Puzzle # 108

R			O	I				L
	L	I			A			
O	E	A					I	R
	A		M			O	F	D
		O			E			
I	D	R			F		A	
A	O	E				D	L	F
			F			R	M	
M				A	D			O

"A _____ ___ the book's". The Democratic-Republicans won a sweeping victory in 1800. But an unusual problem arose. According to the constitution, members of the Electoral College were to vote for two candidates, without indicating which office each one was to fill. The person receiving the most votes was to become President, and the runner-up to be vice president. The Democratic-Republicans had nominated Jefferson for president and Aaron Burr for vice president. Since each elector cast two votes for his party's candidates, the result was a tie, between Jefferson and Burr.

Clue Word _ _ _ _ _ _ _ _ _

Puzzle # 109

The Constitution of the United States of America _____ ___ solution that when two candidates are tied in the Electoral College, the House of Representatives must choose between them. Jefferson was the Democratic-Republicans' choice for president, but Federalist congressmen tried to swing the election to Burr because he was broken by Hamilton. Although a Federalist, he declared himself in favor of Jefferson. Hamilton felt Burr was dangerous and not to be trusted. Hamilton's support of Jefferson influenced the House to choose Jefferson. (Three Years later Burr killed himself in a duel)

	P	D	V	E				R
A			D	S	I			
	O		P		R	E		I
	V		A			O		
E	A						I	V
		O			E		P	
D		V	E		A		R	
			S	I	D			E
O				P	V	S	A	

Clue Word _ _ _ _ _ _ _ _ _

Puzzle # 110

Jefferson was one of the best-educated and most versatile men ever to be president. _____ _____ servant he was had written the Declaration of Independence and served as governor of Virginia, foreign diplomat, secretary of state, and vice president. In addition, he was an inventor, a musician, a scientific farmer, and an architect. He designed both the University of Virginia and his home, in Monticello.

H	L	E		T				
			B	C	P		L	
	C	P	E	L	N		I	
C	E		L		T	H		
T								L
		U	I		E		T	P
	U		P	E		T	H	
	H		T	I	B			
				U		B	P	I

Clue Word _ _ _ _ _ _ _ _ _

Puzzle # 111

	R		Z		I	T		O
I				R	T	E		H
		H	E	U	A		I	
		I	H		R			T
		O				R		
Z			I		O	H		
	O		R	A	Z	I		
U		A	T	I				E
R		I	U		E		H	

Clue Word _ _ _ _ _ _ _ _ _

Puzzle # 112

Jefferson has less success in limiting Federalist influence on the judicial branch of the government. Shortly before federalists left office, congress passed the; "Judiciary Act of 1801" which did _____ an increase in the number of Federal judges. By filling these positions with 'their' supporters, the federalists hoped to keep control of the Judiciary. In his last hours as president, Adams worked far into the night signing appointments to the new positions. The newly appointed officials thus became known as….. "Midnight judges."

L	E	C		O				I
	S	A	N			T	E	
	T		E		L			
		O			A		I	E
T			N					L
I	N		C		O			
		N		S		L		
	O	L		E	I	C		
E						A	O	

In 1801 the ruler of Tripoli demanded higher tribute from the United States to stop the pirates of the four Barbary States of Morocco from seizing foreign ships passing through the Mediterranean, who would loot cargoes and hold crews for ransom. When Jefferson refused, Tripoli declared war. Jefferson then sent a few ships to blockade that country's _____. A young naval lieutenant named Stephen Decatur performed the most daring deed of the war. One night, he sneaked into the Harbor of Tripoli and destroyed an American vessel that had been captured and converted into a warship. In 1805 a treaty was signed for peace.

Clue Word _ _ _ _ _ _ _ _

Puzzle # 113

The most significant event of Jefferson's presidency is when he "_____" Louisiana. At this time, the term referred to a vast territory lying between the Mississippi River and the Rocky Mountains. France had originally claimed Louisiana ceded the region to Spain at the end of the French and Indian War. But when Napoleon rose to power in France in the 1790s, he wanted to restore the French empire in America. In 1800, he forced Spain to return Louisiana to France. Therefore, Jefferson didn't want Napoleon's troops at our back door and decided to buy New Orleans from the French early in 1803.

	H	R	A	S				E
			P		E	A	U	
E			C					R
	P		E		R		C	
S		C	H		P	D		A
	U		D		S		R	
R					C			S
	E	H	S		D			
C				E	A	U	H	

Clue Word _ _ _ _ _ _ _ _ _

Puzzle # 114

However, by 1803 Napoleon's situation changed and the French ruler had given up his dream of an Empire in America. He had lost thousands of French troops in trying to crush 2 slave rebellions, France was again on the verge of war with England and needed money. Napoleon surprised Livingston & Monroe by offering to sell Louisiana… Including New Orleans for only $15 Million. Seizing the chance to buy this territory at so ____ __ _____, the Americans accepted Napoleon's offer. The original offer by Monroe & Livingston was $10 million for Just New Orleans in 1803. Jefferson got the whole 'territory' (Now a State) for 5 Million more.

O					A	I		P
R				W		A	O	
A		E	O					
	O	A	L	I		P	C	W
	C			O			A	
L	R			A	W	O	E	
					C	W		O
	A			L				R
W		R	R					A

Clue Word _ _ _ _ _ _ _ _ _

Puzzle # 115

			N		G			O
	E	I	R		L	N		
	G			I	O			L
			X	N	P	L		R
R								X
X		N	L	E	R			
P			I	R			G	
		X	G		N	I	L	
I			P		X			

Clue Word _ _ _ _ _ _ _ _ _

In 1804, Jefferson needed Meriwether Lewis and William Clark to do the _____ of what was now called "The Louisiana Purchase?" The Northern part of the purchase. Their expedition started from ST. Louis and followed the Mississippi River to its source. The group crossed the Rocky Mountains into the area known as the Oregon Country and then followed the Columbia River to the Pacific Ocean. The explorers were sided during their two-year journey by an Indian tracker named: --- SACAJAWED.

Puzzle # 116

James Madison succeeded Jefferson as president in 1809. For the next three years, he tried to protect American neutrality by using economic pressure against Britain, to no avail. The British continued to interfere with U.S. ships, impress American seamen, and violate the nation's neutral rights and coastal waters. American seamen and Americans by the middle of 1812, and anti-British feelings were so strong in the United States that Madison asked Congress to declare war against Britain. It did so in June. Through the war _____ _____ two years, it is known as the war of 1812.

Clue Word _ _ _ _ _ _ _ _ _

Puzzle # 117

_____ ___ _____, numbering 16 vessels, was hopelessly outclassed by the British fleet of more than 1000 warships - The largest navy in the world. Even so, the Americans scored several outstanding victories against the British. (Britain was once again at war with France, which helped the United States.) The warship "constitution", commanded by Isaac Hall destroyed the British warship "Guerrier" in a furious battle. These victories made with the constitution and 'Old Ironsides' and "The United States" commanded by Stephen Decatur, captured the "Macedonian", Altogether, U.S. Naval vessels and privateers seized or destroyed almost 1500 British merchant vessels during the war.

Clue Word _ _ _ _ _ _ _ _ _

Puzzle # 118

"We have met the enemy, and they are ours"
Oliver Hazard reporting his victory _____
_____ Battle of Lake Erie.

	E	D	N		I		H	
H	I			D			U	
	R	N	U		R		I	G
							N	R
		R		E		I		
G	D							
R	G		D		H	U	T	
	T			R			G	D
	N		I		G	H	R	

Clue Word _ _ _ _ _ _ _ _ _

Puzzle # 119

A		C			U	E		
			A	R			P	B
P	B			C		Y		
	U			T	A			
E		T				U		Y
			C	U			B	
		B		P			E	C
C	T		A	Y				
		A	R			B		T

"Don't give up the ship" last words of James Lawrence, dying captain of the American warship "Chesapeake" before its _____ ___ the British.

Clue Word _ _ _ _ _ _ _ _ _

Puzzle # 120

U				T			
E	T	S	A				
V	G	A		I	S		T
	I		G	T			
		V	P		S	T	
			A	E		U	
P		G	I		E	T	S
				V	A	P	I
		S					V

The battle of Lake Champlain in September 1814, about 11,000 British troops, moving South from Canada invaded New York along the western shore of Lake Champlain. Battle of the British and the Americans had ships on the lake. The two fleets met in the battle of Lake Champlain. The American fleet, commanded by Thomas McDonough, skillfully outmaneuvered the British and defeated them completely. With its naval support gone, the British army retreated to Canada and _____ ___ ____ invasion of New York.

Clue Word _ _ _ _ _ _ _ _ _

Puzzle # 121

Meanwhile, a _____ ___ British warships had entered Chesapeake Bay and landed troops in Maryland. They marched into Washington, D.C., almost unopposed. Retaliating for the destruction of York by American Raiders, the year before, the British set fire to many government buildings. Among them were the capital and the White House. Shortly thereafter, the British withdrew from the city.

	O		B				A
E			A	O	F	B	G
		G	E			F	
		D		A			O
F		A	G		O	R	E
O				F		I	
	F				A	G	
D		I	O	B	G		F
G					I		R

Clue Word _ _ _ _ _ _ _ _ _

Puzzle # 122

_____ ___ Lake Champlain and in the Chesapeake Bay, the British next moved against New Orleans. From bases in the Caribbean, they transported some 7500 troops to Louisiana late in 1814. Led by Andrew Jackson, the American frontiersmen defending New Orleans put up to a barricade and awaited the enemy. On January 8, 1815, the British attacked, in the battle that followed. They were thoroughly beaten, and they suffered over 2000 casualties at the hands of sharp shooting westerners. U.S. losses numbered 71 killed or wounded.

	L			A	D		E	T
		E	C		T			K
	T	D	E					
	O					E	B	
K		B		C		D		L
	C	L					K	
					B	C	L	
L			D		C	O		
E	B		A	L			T	

Clue Word _ _ _ _ _ _ _ _ _

Puzzle # 123

	H		T	A	1			L
E		L		H		A		
		1	E		L			
T	R		L		Y			A
		E				L		
H			R		T		Y	9
			9		E	Y		
		H		Y		1		T
A			1	T	H		L	

Clue Word _ _ _ _ _ _ _ _ _

In the _____ ____ century, Spain controlled an important area south of the United States. One part of it, known as "East Florida", was the long Peninsula into the Atlantic. The other part called "West Florida", was a narrow stretch of land extending west along the Gulf of Mexico to the Mississippi River. The United States claimed that a large portion of West Florida was included in the Louisiana Purchase. When American colonists North of New Orleans declared independence from Spanish rule in 1810, the United States annexed this section. Three years later, during the war of 1812, American troops captured the Spanish Ford at Mobile. The Americans kept this part of West Florida, too, despite Spain's protests.

Puzzle # 124

Americans _____ was about Spanish control of "East Florida". Indians escaped to the area after attacking Southern settlements. Runaway slaves fled there, too. And pirates and smugglers used the base of Florida to hide. In 1818 Andrew Jackson was sent to subdue some semitone Indians who had been raiding settlements in Alabama and Georgia. He pursued the Indians into East Florida, defeated them, and also captured several Spanish Forts. His expedition made it clear that the United States could take all of East Florida by force if it wanted to. In 1819, Spain agreed to give up the region. In exchange, the United States agreed to cancel Spain's $ 5 million debt to American citizens. The Spaniards also surrendered their rights to West Florida. The United States in turn, gave up its claim to Texas.

L			I		M			
C	T		L		P	A		
	M	P		T		N		
N			T	P		O		
	I		A		N		T	
		L		I	O			N
	N		L		I	O		
	A	N		T			L	M
		M		I				E

Clue Word _ _ _ _ _ _ _ _ _

Puzzle # 125

Meanwhile, another development threatened the Pacific Coast. Russia, starting from its base in Alaska, began to expand southward. In 1821, the Russians claimed the Pacific Coast as for South as the parallel, within the Oregon Country. Americans did not like the idea of European intervention in the Western Hemisphere. In 1823, President Monroe issued a strong warning to Europe to keep out. This proclamation was defined in ___ _____ later called the Monroe Doctrine which became a cornerstone of U.S. foreign policy. 1) The American Continents were closed to further colonization by European nations. 2) Any attempt by any European powers to interference with American Government would be considered as unfriendly and against the United States. 3) The United States would not interference in European affairs or with existing colonies in the Western Hemisphere.

	A			N	E		I	
	D				O	R	E	N
	C	N			R			O
		D	O		A	N		
A				E				R
		E	D		T	A		
N			E			D		
I	T	A	R				N	
	E		N	A			O	

Clue Word _ _ _ _ _ _ _ _ _

Puzzle # 126

_____ _____ early 19th Century, the United States changes a great deal. Its size doubled, and its population quadrupled. Industrialization began to reshape the nation's economy. A French visitors in the 1830's described the United States as "A Land of Wonders" where "everything is in constant motion and every change seems as improvement."

U		N		T	D			
	H	R		N				
D	G	T						N
	I		E		T			
		D		H		I		
			N		I		G	
H						U	N	I
			T		H	D		
			I	G		E		T

Clue Word _ _ _ _ _ _ _ _ _ _

Puzzle # 127

One of the first Trans-Appalachians regions to be settled ____ ____ ____ southwest, the area south of the Ohio River. (It is called the Old Southwest to differentiate it from the "newer" Southwest beyond the Mississippi.)

		L	E		H	S	W	D
				D				
H			T		S	A		O
	T	E	D	S			O	
		W				T		
		O		W			D	S
O		H	S		W			T
				T				
D	S	T	L		E	W		

Clue Word _ _ _ _ _ _ _ _ _ _

Puzzle # 128

O	T	A		S		N		W
	G				A			
		N				S	A	
	S				W	T		G
T	A		N		G		O	S
G		E	R				N	
	E	T				G		
			G				T	
W		G		A		E	S	O

The most famous pioneer in this _____ ____ Daniel Boone. One of the first to explore Kentucky, he found a pathway across the Appalachians through the Cumberland Gap. This was the Wilderness Road, which became the main route for migration into the territory.

Clue Word _ _ _ _ _ _ _ _ _

Puzzle # 129

James Harrods was to establish the first pioneer settlement in Kentucky at Harrods burg in 1774. Boones borough was founded the following years by settlers led in by Boone. James Robertson, an early settler of the Watauga Valley in Tennessee founded Nashville in 1780. _____ _____, there were some 109,000 in Kentucky and Tennessee. The settler population grew to nearly 327,000 by 1800 and to more than 1.6 million by 1840.

			A	F		1		
A		T						
O	R		T		7		A	
		R	E	7		9		
T								1
	F		O	R	T			
	T		7		1		9	O
						R		E
		E		R	F			

Clue Word _ _ _ _ _ _ _ _ _

Puzzle # 130

Further south, the old Southwest was _____ as the Mississippi territory. It was opened to settlement in 1798. Southern planters moved there with their slaves and developed large cotton plantations in the fertile low lands. Indians, however, hindered settlement in the region until Andrew Jackson's victory at Horseshoe. Bend in 1814, thousands of Southern then gave up their worn-out farms in the Carolinas and Georgia and headed southwest. The population of the region was about 41,000 in 1810, and more than 200,000 ten years later, and almost 1 million by 1840.

					Z	G		R
	E		G		N			
	I		R					E
N			Z		I		G	
	O		D			R		
G		A		E				N
A					G		Z	
		N		O		A		
I		Z	D					

Clue Word _____

Puzzle # 131

T					H	F		
O							T	A
N	E		D					
H	T	A		O				
			F		D			
			A		O	L	N	
				O			E	D
A	H							O
		O						T

Clue Word _____

The ordinance of 1785 as a law provided that the land was to be surveyed and divided into Townships six miles square. Each township was to contain 36 sections one mile square (640 Acres). One section in each township was set aside for the support of Public Schools. The rest ___ ____ _____ was then offered for sale at public Auction at a minimum price of $ 1.00 an Acre. A purchaser had to buy a full section of land. Since most settlers could not afford to do this, land companies bought up much of the region. They subdivided the section and sold the smaller lots to settlers at a point.

Puzzle # 132

Z			G				E	I
		I		D	E			
A		D	I					N
	R			A	D			
	O	N				G	A	
			R	G			O	
R					O			G
			E	I		E		
E	I				R	A		

The ordinance of 1787 as a law, is often called the "North West Ordinance". It _____ the old Northwest into the Northwest Territory and provided a plan for governing it. The law includes six provisions. (1) Congress would set up a temporary government by appointing a governor & 3 Judges. (2) When the territory had 5000 free adult males, a representative legislature was established. (3) When 60,000 were free as settlers the region would be eligible for admission into the union as a state, (4) Personal rights, religion, speech, and trial by jury were all guaranteed. (5) Slavery was prohibited (6) Public Schools were encouraged.

Clue Word _ _ _ _ _ _ _ _ _

Puzzle # 133

Usually, the first people into a large region were scouts and fur traders. They were single men - "loners" who liked independence. Next came the speculators. They bought large tracts of land to subdivide and sell to pioneer farmers. The first farm families in the West _____

_____ as the earliest settlers had along the Atlantic Coast. The men hacked clearings out of the wilderness, built simple log cabins, and raised food for their families. Pioneer women were skilled at preserving food, making clothes, and using home remedies to cure sickness and to help protect their families from Indian or Invaders.

	H				U			D
		M				I		L
		I		C		H		
	I					L	D	H
		U		E				
M	C	D					E	
		V		M		D		
E		N			D			
C			L				M	

Clue Word _ _ _ _ _ _ _ _ _

Puzzle # 134

From the settler's point of view, the Native Americans were holding back the March of all civilization by their resistance to the spread of farms and towns. From the Native Americans' point of view, the settlers were destroying their way of life ____ _____ of food by cutting down forests and lolling off wild game.

R		D	C					U
			D				R	E
	O	U						
C	R			E				
			O		R			
				A			U	D
						C	A	
S	D				A			
E					N	O		R

Clue Word _ _ _ _ _ _ _ _ _

Puzzle # 135

A				N				U
	R	G					N	
					P	I		R
	M	R	P					
	U		M		R		P	
				F	R	I		
U		F	G					
	G					A	U	
M				U				F

Clue Word _ _ _ _ _ _ _ _ _

Thousands of Native Americans chose to move west of the Mississippi, where few settlers lived. Others were forcibly moved. This happened in the South East during the 1830's. The Native American inhabitants of the area - the Cherokees, the Chickasaws, Choctaws, creeks, and the Seminoles - were known as the "five civilized tribes". They had taken ___ _____ and were making a serious effort to adapt to the culture of their white neighbors but to no avail. Against their will, they were driven from their lands and marched to what is now Oklahoma. So many died on this journey it is still today called, "The Trail of Tears."

Puzzle # 136

Before the Industrial Revolution came to America, almost everyone lived in rural areas. The spread of Industrialization changed this. _____ were usually built in or near cities, or cities grew up around new _____. As more and more Americans gained employment as "factory" workers, they also became city dwellers. Between 1800 and 1840, the number of American cities that could boast a population of 10,000 or more rose from 6 to 37.

	E		O				T	
		C	T	S				I
		T	A		C		E	
		R						
S				I				C
					E			
	O		C		R	F		
A				T	O	S		
	I				F		C	

Clue Word _ _ _ _ _ _ _ _ _

Puzzle # 137

_____ also began to aid American farmers in the early 1800's. For a long time, farming methods had been crude and unscientific. In 1800, most farmers were still using simple tools to work their land. Every step in farming, from planting to harvesting, was done by hand. The most important invention in this period was probably Eli Whitney's cotton gin; (short for 'engine'), which was introduced in 1793. It was a simple machine that separated seeds from the cotton fibers 50 times faster than the process could be done by hand. Other new or improved implements for farming were introduced early in the 19th century.

		N	H	M				
							I	
	A	C		N		E		
C		R	N					E
M			E		I			H
H					C	I		Y
		E		H		A	Y	
	M							
				E	A	M		

Clue Word _ _ _ _ _ _ _ _

Puzzle # 138

As the United States increased in size, it needed improved networks for transportation, Industries wanted better and faster ways to get raw materials ____ ___ _____ finished products to market. Land vehicles of the early 19th century, pulled by Horses, were slow and hard to handle. The chief means of carrying passengers and mail was the stagecoach. For transporting freight, Americans developed the Conestoga wagon. It was canvas-covered, with a high body, board-rimmed wheels, and a water-tight bottom for crossing streams.

T								D
				S	I	N		
S		D		P			O	
	T		S	I		N		
D		O				S		I
		S		T	O		A	
	P			A		H		S
	D	I	T					
O								A

Clue Word _ _ _ _ _ _ _ _ _

Puzzle # 139

The first development in land transportation after the Revolutionary War was building _____. These were toll roads constructed by private companies for profit. _____ got their name from a "pike" (pole) across the road was turned aside after a traveler had paid the toll.

	R							
		E	N		S			
	E		I			U		T
E	N			K				R
S			N		R			E
P				U			S	N
N		T			U		P	
		P		T	S			
							K	

Clue Word _ _ _ _ _ _ _ _ _

Puzzle # 140

		O		L		D	I
E	L	G					
D			Y		G		W
	T	Y		G			
G		W				T		Y
				L		I	G
	W		L		D			G
					W	I	E
T	G		W				

Roads helped in transporting goods, but overland hauling was still expensive. Since water travel was cheaper, rivers and lakes ____ _____ issued wherever such inland waterways existed. The Ohio River, for instance, was the major route for settlers moving into the Northwest Territory. To connect bodies of water, Americans built a network of Canals. One such popular Canal built by Americans was the "Erie Canal" built in 1817 under the leadership of Dewitt Clinton, Governor of New York, which stretched 363 miles of waterway.

Clue Word _ _ _ _ _ _ _ _ _

Puzzle # 141

As in many other aspects of the Industrial Revolution, the British pioneered in development of a practical steam locomotive. They also built ____ _____ first railroad in the 1820's. Americans were not far behind, the first railroads in the United States were opened to traffic in the 1830's. Among the earliest lines were the Baltimore and Ohio and the Mohawk and Hudson. Operating between Albany and Schenectady, New York. By 1840, nearly 3000 miles of track were in use.

W	L					R		
	T			L			E	D
H			T	D				
S					R			
		T	D		O	L		
		H					R	
			H	D			L	
L	S			T			D	
	O					S	T	

Clue Word _ _ _ _ _ _ _ _ _

Puzzle # 142

Two events in Europe stimulated immigration in the 1840's. One was the failure of the potato crop in Ireland. Deprived of their main source of food, thousands of Irish starved to death. Thousands more fled to the United States as their only hope for survival. The second event was a series of unsuccessful uprisings ___ _____ against their rulers in 1848. Fearing imprisonment or other punishment, many Germans left their homeland and came to the United States.

R						M		
B	A				E			
		G		N	A	E		
Y			N	B				
N								Y
				M	R			S
	Y	M	B		G			
		R					S	G
		G						A

Clue Word _ _ _ _ _ _ _ _ _

Puzzle # 143

	U	1		T	2			4
T								N
		B	4		U			
B	T	2						
		8				1		
						T	I	B
			T		1	U		
2								8
I			2	B		4	T	

Clue Word _ _ _ _ _ _ _ _ _

Andrew Jackson was a dominant figure of the early 19th century. His military record during the War of 1812 made him a national hero. He added to his reputation with his campaign against the Seminoles and the Spaniards in Florida. Later, he served as governor of the newly acquired territory of Florida and then as a U.S. Senator. Aiming for the presidency, he tried for it unsuccessfully ___ _____ ____ won in 1828. He also chose his successor in 1836. Jackson had a strong character, a colorful personality, and firm beliefs. The period of his influence in American History is often called the "Age of Jackson" or "The Jacksonian Era".

Puzzle # 144

	7	8	1					E
	F		7					9
			8		E			A
				E		A		F
		E				R		
7		1		9				
R			9		8			
1					F		E	
T					R	8	F	

In the original 13 States, only a minority of citizens were permitted to vote. All the states had some sort of property qualification for voting. An adult more could vote or hold only if he owned land or paid taxes. Women and slaves could not vote, not could free blacks in most states. The new states that joined the union _____ _____ were more democratic. Most of them allowed all adult white males to vote and hold office.

Clue Word _ _ _ _ _ _ _ _ _

Puzzle # 145

As Jackson served the end of his second term, he persuaded the _____ to nominate his personal choice for the presidency. The candidate he selected was his longtime adviser, MARTIN VAN BUREN of New York. Van Buren had been vice president in Jackson's second administration. He won the election in 1836.

A	D	S						
			C	O				T
		C	S					
D	C		T					
	S			M			E	
					E	E	S	R
M		R		O	O			
			A	S	S			
							M	E

Clue Word _ _ _ _ _ _ _ _ _

Puzzle # 146

The Democrats nominated Van Buren for a second term in 1840. But many blamed him for the country's _____ _____. Van Buren had other problems as well. The Whigs staged a colorful campaign to promote their candidate.

R	T	M			E			
		D	S	H		T		
						M	A	
		E		A		I		T
T			M		I			A
M		A		T		R		
	E	I						
	M		R		A			
			E			A	H	M

Clue Word _ _ _ _ _ _ _ _ _

Puzzle # 147

M	O			L			H	
T					I			E
H			E	N	O			
				I	M		N	
		T		W		H		
	M		N	O				
		O	E	T				H
W			H					N
	H					W	T	

Clue Word _ _ _ _ _ _ _ _ _

"John Marshall has made his decision; ____ ____ ____ enforce it." Andrew Jackson commenting on the Supreme Court decision on Worcester V. Georgia.

Puzzle # 148

	P		C					
		I	B			N		P
	U		A	I				B
I						D	P	
		P				C		
	L	C						I
B				C	I		A	
A		L			N	P		
					B		D	

Many people of the early 1800's felt that excessive drinking was a cause of misfortune in society. The amount of Alcohol consumed in the United States was indeed very great. Drunkenness was common at almost every _____ ____ private celebration. The first anti-drinking organization in the United States was formed in 1808.

Clue Word _ _ _ _ _ _ _ _ _

Puzzle # 149

Several new or expanding religious groups attracted members in the early 1800's. One new denomination was the Disciples of Christ (known today as the Christian Church), which _____ _____ the Presbyterians. Another new group was to play a prominent role in American history. It was called the Church of Jesus Christ of Latter-day Saints, or Mormons. Joseph Smith founded the denomination in upstate New York in 1830. He reported that an Angel had guided him to a set of golden plates, which Smith translated as the Book of Mormon.

M		R	T					S
				F		P		
	P		L				T	
	R			M			S	T
		L		F		O		
S	M			R			F	
	O				S		M	
	F		I					
L					M	I		R

Clue Word _ _ _ _ _ _ _ _ _

Puzzle # 150

The communities of the early 19th century affected few Americans. But many found their lives _____ ___ the growth of manufacturing. The factory system was giving rise to an American laboring class- people who depended on wages for a living. Their work conditions were grim. Men, women, and children usually worked from dawn to dusk, six days a week in buildings that were often uncomfortable, and even very dangerous. The average pay for men was about $5.00 a week. Women earned less than half as much & children as little as $1.00 a week.

G					Y	A		B
E	A	Y					H	
				G	A			
	Y	A					C	
			A	C	G			
	N					E	D	
			N	H				
	E					N	Y	D
A		N	B					H

Clue Word _ _ _ _ _ _ _ _ _

Puzzle # 151

C			I				B	
						E	O	U
	D				O			
		U	O		E		I	N
		A			C			
O	E		N		I	U		
			T				C	
D	O	T						
A	U				N			A

Clue Word _ _ _ _ _ _ _ _ _

One of the most outstanding figures in America was Horace Mann. A Massachusetts lawyer, he supervised the State's public _____ system, from 1837 to 1848. He persuaded the state of Massachusetts to set aside more money for schools and teachers' salaries and to increase the number of subjects taught. The school year was extended from a few weeks to six months, so new high schools were opened. Under Mann's guidance, the first American school for the training of teachers was established at Lexington, Massachusetts, in 1839.

Puzzle # 152

SOLUTIONS

E	H	S	L	P	A	T	I	N
L	P	A	I	T	N	H	S	E
T	N	I	S	H	E	L	P	A
A	E	L	H	I	S	N	T	P
I	T	P	N	E	L	S	A	H
N	S	H	P	A	T	E	L	I
P	L	E	T	N	I	A	H	S
S	I	N	A	L	N	P	E	T
H	A	T	E	S	P	I	N	L

Clue Word : THE PLAINS   PUZZLE#1

S	U	O	H	F	B	I	T	R
I	H	B	R	T	U	O	F	S
F	T	R	I	O	S	B	U	H
R	B	H	U	S	T	F	I	O
O	I	U	F	B	H	S	R	T
T	S	F	O	I	R	H	B	U
B	R	I	S	H	F	H	O	I
U	O	S	B	R	I	T	H	F
H	F	I	T	U	O	R	S	B

Clue Word : BIRTHOFUS   PUZZLE#2

I	R	Y	E	V	D	S	C	O
O	V	C	S	I	Y	D	R	E
D	S	E	R	C	O	I	Y	V
R	I	D	V	E	S	C	O	Y
C	O	V	Y	D	I	E	S	R
Y	E	S	O	R	C	V	D	I
S	C	R	I	Y	E	O	V	D
E	Y	O	D	S	V	R	I	C
V	D	I	C	O	R	Y	E	S

Clue Word : DISCOVERY   PUZZLE#3

T	E	H	X	U	M	L	S	A
S	U	L	H	A	T	X	M	E
X	A	M	L	S	E	T	H	U
U	H	X	S	M	A	E	L	T
A	L	T	E	X	H	M	U	S
M	S	E	U	T	L	H	A	X
E	X	A	M	H	S	U	T	L
H	T	U	A	L	X	S	E	M
L	M	S	T	E	U	A	X	H

Clue Word : THE UXMALS   PUZZLE#4

I	N	C	Z	T	E	K	A	D
T	A	D	C	I	K	E	N	Z
E	Z	K	A	N	D	I	T	C
N	K	T	I	A	Z	C	D	E
A	C	Z	E	D	T	N	I	K
D	E	I	N	K	C	A	Z	T
Z	D	A	K	C	I	T	E	N
C	I	E	T	Z	N	D	K	A
K	T	N	D	E	A	Z	C	I

Clue Word : AZTEC KIND   PUZZLE#5

S	C	I	A	E	U	N	P	R
P	R	E	S	C	N	I	A	U
A	U	N	P	R	I	C	E	S
U	N	R	I	S	E	A	C	P
C	I	A	N	P	R	U	S	E
E	P	S	U	A	C	R	N	I
N	A	U	E	I	S	P	R	C
R	E	P	C	U	A	S	I	N
I	S	C	R	N	P	E	U	A

Clue Word : PERUINCAS   PUZZLE#6

E	M	B	U	L	P	S	O	I
S	L	I	B	O	E	M	U	P
U	P	O	M	S	I	L	B	E
I	U	E	S	B	M	P	L	O
L	S	M	P	I	O	B	E	U
O	B	P	E	U	L	I	M	S
B	O	U	L	P	S	E	I	M
M	I	S	O	E	B	U	P	L
P	E	L	I	M	U	O	S	B

Clue Word : MI PUEBIOS   PUZZLE#7

E	A	R	V	P	N	U	S	I
V	N	P	I	S	U	R	A	E
I	S	U	R	A	E	V	N	P
S	R	N	A	U	P	E	I	V
P	U	E	S	I	V	N	R	A
A	I	V	N	E	R	S	P	U
N	V	I	U	R	A	P	E	S
U	E	S	P	N	I	A	V	R
R	P	A	E	V	S	I	U	N

Clue Word : PERUVIANS   PUZZLE#8

PUZZLE#9

S	G	U	N	H	A	D	U	O
A	M	N	O	G	D	S	M	H
O	D	H	S	U	M	N	A	G
M	S	A	H	N	G	U	O	D
D	H	O	M	S	U	G	N	A
N	U	G	A	D	O	H	S	M
H	O	S	G	M	N	A	D	U
U	N	M	D	A	H	O	G	S
G	A	D	U	O	S	M	H	N

Clue Word : MUD HOGANS

PUZZLE#10

H	N	A	U	S	T	O	K	E
S	U	O	R	H	E	T	N	A
R	T	R	N	O	A	H	S	U
A	H	S	T	U	O	R	E	N
T	O	N	E	R	S	A	U	H
E	R	U	A	N	H	S	T	O
P	A	R	S	E	U	N	H	T
U	S	W	O	T	N	E	A	R
N	E	T	H	A	R	U	O	S

Clue Word : A SOUTHERN

PUZZLE#11

B	M	N	A	D	E	O	C	I
C	O	D	B	N	I	A	E	M
I	A	E	O	C	M	B	D	N
M	B		I	A	N	D	O	E
D	N	O	M	E	B	C	I	A
A	E	I	C	O	D	M	N	B
N	C	A	E	M	O	I	B	D
E	I	M	D	B	C	N	A	O
O	D	B	N	I	A	E	M	C

Clue Word : BE NOMADIC

PUZZLE#12

I	G	B	R	E	H	T	N	U
N	U	E	T	G	B	H	I	R
H	T	R	I	N	U	B	G	E
R	I	H	B	T	N	U	E	G
T	E	G	U	I	R	N	H	B
B	N	U	E	N	G	I	R	T
U	B	N	H	R	E	G	T	I
E	H	T	G	B	I	R	U	N
G	R	I	N	U	T	E	B	H

Clue Word : BIG HUNTER

N	H	M	D	E	S	T	A	O
O	T	A	M	H	N	D	E	S
D	S	E	T	A	O	M	H	N
S	A	O	H	D	E	N	T	M
M	N	T	O	S	A	E	D	H
H	E	D	N	T	M	S	O	A
E	O	N	A	M	T	H	S	D
T	M	H	S	O	D	A	N	E
A	D	S	E	N	H	O	M	T

Clue Word : THE NOMADS   PUZZLE#13

A	I	W	O	R	K	B	S	N
O	S	N	W	A	B	K	R	I
B	R	K	I	N	S	A	O	W
W	B	A	R	K	O	N	I	S
N	K	R	S	I	A	O	W	B
I	O	S	B	W	N	R	K	A
K	W	B	A	O	I	S	N	R
S	N	I	K	B	R	W	A	O
R	A	O	H	S	W	I	B	K

Clue Word : WORK BASIN   PUZZLE#14

O	H	N	T	1	R	W	E	I
E	1	W	N	I	O	H	R	T
T	R	I	H	W	E	N	O	1
R	I	T	O	N	1	E	H	W
H	W	1	E	R	T	I	N	O
N	E	O	W	H	I	T	1	R
W	T	E	R	O	H	1	I	N
I	O	H	1	T	N	R	W	E
1	N	R	I	E	W	O	T	H

Clue Word : THEIR OWN 1   PUZZLE#15

H	S	T	H	U	M	E	A	P
A	M	U	P	T	E	S	H	H
P	E	H	H	A	S	T	M	U
S	H	P	A	M	T	U	H	E
H	A	E	U	S	P	M	T	H
U	T	M	E	H	H	P	S	A
E	U	S	T	H	A	H	P	M
M	P	A	S	E	H	H	U	T
T	H	H	M	P	U	A	E	S

Clue Word : THEM HUPAS   PUZZLE#16

H	N	C	I	A	E	Y	P	W
P	Y	E	N	H	W	C	I	A
I	A	W	P	C	Y	N	E	H
A	E	N	Y	P	H	W	C	I
Y	C	P	A	W	I	E	H	N
W	H	I	C	E	N	P	A	Y
N	W	A	E	I	P	H	Y	C
C	P	Y	H	N	A	I	W	E
E	I	H	W	Y	C	A	N	P

Clue Word : CHIPEWYAN　　　　　　　PUZZLE#17

M	O	A	I	D	N	E	K	S
I	N	D	S	K	E	O	A	M
K	E	S	M	O	A	D	I	N
S	A	I	E	N	M	K	A	O
E	M	K	O	A	D	N	S	I
N	D	O	K	S	I	A	M	E
O	K	E	A	M	S	I	N	D
D	I	M	N	E	K	S	O	A
A	S	N	D	I	O	M	E	K

Clue Word : ESKIMOAND　　　　　　　PUZZLE#18

R	N	S	E	O	U	A	E	P
A	E	U	P	N	S	E	R	O
P	E	O	A	R	E	N	S	U
U	A	E	R	P	E	S	O	N
S	R	P	O	E	N	U	E	A
N	O	E	U	S	A	R	P	E
E	S	A	E	U	P	O	N	R
E	U	R	N	E	O	P	A	S
P	P	N	S	A	R	E	U	E

Clue Word : EUROPEANS　　　　　　　PUZZLE#19

W	R	N	A	9	4	D	1	3
A	9	1	W	D	3	R	4	N
D	3	4	1	N	R	9	W	A
3	A	9	R	4	N	1	D	W
N	1	D	3	W	9	4	A	R
4	W	R	D	A	1	3	N	9
9	4	A	N	3	D	W	R	1
R	N	3	4	1	W	A	9	D
1	D	W	9	R	A	N	3	4

Clue Word : DRAWN 1493　　　　　　　PUZZLE#20

Q	E	A	R	O	U	I	T	C
T	R	C	Q	E	I	O	A	U
I	O	U	T	A	C	R	E	Q
R	A	I	C	T	Q	E	U	O
U	Q	T	E	I	O	C	R	A
E	C	O	A	U	R	T	Q	I
A	U	R	I	C	T	Q	O	E
C	T	E	O	Q	A	U	I	R
O	I	Q	U	R	E	A	C	T

Clue Word : TO ACQUIRE   PUZZLE#21

C	O	E	F	Y	G	R	A	L
L	R	F	C	O	A	Y	G	E
Y	G	A	E	R	L	O	F	C
O	Y	G	R	A	C	E	L	F
E	F	L	Y	G	O	C	R	A
R	A	C	L	F	E	G	Y	O
G	L	O	A	C	Y	F	E	R
F	E	Y	O	L	R	A	C	G
A	C	R	G	E	F	L	O	Y

Clue Word : LEGACY FOR   PUZZLE#22

L	1	8	C	I	M	2	A	6
C	6	A	1	2	8	L	M	I
M	2	I	A	6	L	C	1	8
2	L	6	8	A	1	I	C	M
1	A	C	2	M	I	8	6	L
8	I	M	6	L	C	1	2	A
I	8	2	M	C	A	6	L	1
A	C	1	L	8	6	M	I	2
6	M	L	I	1	2	A	8	C

Clue Word : 1682 CLAIM   PUZZLE#23

N	G	I	S	H	E	O	L	F
L	F	O	G	N	I	S	H	E
E	S	H	O	L	F	G	N	I
S	L	N	F	G	H	I	E	O
H	I	E	N	O	S	L	F	G
G	O	F	I	E	L	H	S	N
O	H	S	E	F	G	N	I	L
F	N	L	H	I	O	E	G	S
I	E	G	L	S	N	F	O	H

Clue Word : ENGLISH OF   PUZZLE#24

I	U	H	G	T	N	R	D	E
G	T	R	D	E	U	H	I	N
N	D	E	I	H	R	U	G	T
U	I	G	E	R	H	T	N	D
R	E	D	N	G	T	I	U	H
H	N	T	U	D	I	E	R	G
T	H	N	R	U	D	G	E	I
D	G	U	T	I	E	N	H	R
E	R	I	H	N	G	D	T	U

Clue Word : DURING THE   PUZZLE#25

I	K	O	H	F	T	N	E	G
H	E	F	G	N	O	I	T	K
T	G	N	K	E	I	F	O	H
N	F	T	I	O	G	K	H	E
K	O	G	N	H	E	T	I	F
E	I	H	T	K	F	G	N	O
O	H	K	F	I	N	E	G	T
F	T	I	E	G	H	O	K	N
G	N	E	O	T	K	H	F	I

Clue Word : THE KING OF   PUZZLE#26

B	H	E	F	R	R	S	O	I
F	R	O	I	S	B	H	R	E
R	I	S	O	E	H	B	F	R
S	R	I	B	H	O	E	R	F
O	B	H	R	F	E	R	I	S
E	F	R	S	R	I	O	B	H
I	O	F	H	B	S	R	E	R
R	S	R	E	O	F	I	H	B
H	E	B	R	I	R	F	S	O

Clue Word : FROBISHER   PUZZLE#27

J	S	N	W	E	O	M	T	A
A	E	W	J	M	T	S	N	O
O	T	M	A	S	N	J	E	W
S	N	A	E	O	J	T	W	M
W	J	T	M	N	S	O	A	E
M	O	E	T	W	A	N	J	S
E	W	J	S	T	M	A	O	N
N	A	S	O	J	W	E	M	T
T	M	O	N	A	E	W	S	J

Clue Word : JAMESTOWN   PUZZLE#28

Y	T	S	P	U	M	L	H	O
P	U	M	O	H	L	S	Y	T
H	O	L	S	Y	T	M	P	Y
M	Y	T	U	P	H	O	S	L
U	P	H	L	O	S	Y	T	M
S	L	O	M	T	Y	P	U	H
L	H	Y	T	M	P	U	O	S
T	M	U	Y	S	O	H	L	P
O	S	P	H	L	U	T	M	Y

Clue Word : PLYMOUTHS   PUZZLE#29

W	L	A	Y	M	F	R	E	O
M	Y	O	L	R	E	A	W	F
F	E	R	O	A	W	M	Y	L
Y	A	W	M	F	R	O	L	E
R	M	L	W	E	O	Y	F	A
O	F	E	A	Y	L	W	M	R
A	W	F	R	L	M	E	O	Y
L	R	M	E	O	Y	F	A	W
E	O	Y	F	W	A	L	R	M

Clue Word : MAYFLOWER   PUZZLE#30

E	H	L	O	T	I	N	S	G
G	I	S	L	N	H	O	E	T
T	N	O	G	S	E	H	I	L
I	O	N	S	E	L	T	G	H
H	E	T	I	G	N	L	O	S
L	S	G	H	O	T	I	N	E
O	T	E	N	L	S	G	H	I
N	L	H	E	I	G	S	T	O
S	G	I	T	H	O	E	L	N

Clue Word : TO ENGLISH   PUZZLE#31

E	Y	S	R	F	L	O	A	V
O	R	L	S	A	V	F	E	Y
F	A	V	O	E	Y	S	L	R
R	E	O	V	Y	S	L	F	A
S	V	F	A	L	E	Y	R	O
A	L	Y	F	O	R	E	V	S
V	F	E	Y	S	A	R	O	L
L	S	A	E	R	O	V	Y	F
Y	O	R	L	V	F	A	S	E

Clue Word : OF SLAVERY   PUZZLE#32

B	C	A	L	K	S	H	E	T
H	L	S	C	E	T	A	K	B
K	E	T	B	A	H	C	S	L
E	A	L	H	C	K	T	B	S
C	T	B	A	S	L	E	H	K
S	K	H	T	B	E	L	C	A
T	B	E	S	L	C	K	A	H
L	S	K	E	H	A	B	T	C
A	H	C	K	T	B	S	L	E

Clue Word : THE BLACKS   PUZZLE#33

B	N	Y	R	M	I	F	A	G
R	M	F	A	G	N	Y	B	I
I	G	A	Y	B	F	R	N	M
N	Y	M	B	F	G	I	R	A
G	B	R	N	I	A	M	Y	F
F	A	I	M	R	Y	N	G	B
A	R	G	F	N	M	B	I	Y
Y	F	B	I	A	R	G	M	N
M	I	N	G	Y	B	A	F	R

Clue Word : BY FARMING   PUZZLE#34

T	N	H	W	G	I	A	O	R
I	W	G	R	O	A	H	T	N
A	R	O	T	H	N	I	W	G
O	T	N	H	A	W	G	R	I
G	H	A	I	R	T	O	N	W
W	I	R	G	N	O	T	H	A
H	O	I	N	W	G	R	A	T
R	G	W	A	T	H	N	I	O
N	A	T	O	I	R	W	G	H

Clue Word : GROWTH IN A   PUZZLE#35

C	H	E	T	N	M	S	A	R
N	M	S	R	H	A	T	E	C
A	T	R	E	S	C	M	H	N
S	C	M	A	T	R	E	N	H
R	N	H	M	E	S	A	C	T
T	E	A	N	C	H	R	M	S
E	S	C	H	M	T	N	R	A
M	R	T	C	A	N	H	S	E
H	A	N	S	R	E	C	T	M

Clue Word : MERCHANTS   PUZZLE#36

O	R	F	U	S	T	H	I	A
U	A	I	H	F	O	S	R	T
T	H	S	I	R	A	U	F	O
H	F	U	S	T	I	A	O	R
S	O	T	F	A	R	I	U	H
A	I	R	O	U	H	T	S	F
F	S	O	T	H	U	R	A	I
I	T	A	R	O	S	F	H	U
R	U	H	A	I	F	O	T	S

Clue Word : OUR FAITHS   PUZZLE#37

S	D	R	O	P	E	W	I	H
P	E	W	I	S	H	D	O	R
I	O	H	D	R	W	P	S	E
E	R	D	H	W	S	I	P	O
W	H	S	P	I	O	R	E	D
O	P	I	R	E	D	H	W	S
H	S	P	E	D	I	O	R	W
D	I	E	W	O	R	S	H	P
R	W	O	S	H	P	E	D	I

Clue Word : WORKSHIPED   PUZZLE#38

K	B	U	O	E	T	N	A	W
E	A	T	N	B	W	K	O	U
W	N	O	A	U	K	T	B	E
T	U	W	B	K	N	A	E	O
N	K	A	U	O	E	B	W	T
O	E	B	W	T	A	U	K	N
A	O	K	T	W	U	E	N	B
B	T	N	E	A	O	W	U	K
V	W	E	K	N	B	O	T	A

Clue Word : AWOKEN BUT   PUZZLE#39

A	M	P	I	S	C	N	O	E
C	I	E	N	O	P	S	M	A
N	S	O	G	A	E	I	P	C
O	P	A	R	C	S	M	I	N
E	N	S	E	M	I	A	C	O
M	C	I	O	N	A	P	E	S
S	O	N	P	I	M	E	A	P
I	E	C	D	P	N	O	S	M
P	A	M	T	E	O	C	N	I

Clue Word : COMPANIES   PUZZLE#40

N	L	W	O	D	S	T	E	H
D	H	T	N	W	E	S	L	O
O	S	E	H	T	L	N	W	D
E	D	S	W	H	T	O	N	L
L	T	N	E	O	D	W	H	S
W	O	H	L	S	N	D	T	E
H	E	O	D	N	W	L	S	T
S	W	D	T	L	H	E	O	N
T	N	L	S	E	O	H	D	W

Clue Word : TOWNSHELD   PUZZLE#41

T	A	L	C	H	S	E	O	L
L	H	O	A	T	E	C	L	S
S	C	E	L	O	L	H	A	T
L	E	S	O	L	A	T	C	H
H	T	L	E	L	C	O	S	A
A	O	C	H	S	T	L	E	L
O	L	H	S	C	L	A	T	E
C	L	A	T	E	H	S	L	O
E	S	T	L	A	O	L	H	C

Clue Word : THE LOCALS   PUZZLE#42

T	E	N	D	T	O	U	A	C
D	T	O	A	C	U	N	E	I
C	U	A	N	E	I	D	T	O
E	A	D	O	N	T	I	C	U
T	N	I	C	U	E	O	D	A
O	C	U	I	A	D	E	N	T
U	O	T	E	D	C	A	I	N
A	D	C	U	I	N	T	O	E
N	I	E	T	O	A	C	U	D

Clue Word : EDUCATION   PUZZLE#43

B	E	T	U	J	O	F	C	S
C	U	J	F	T	S	O	E	B
O	S	F	C	B	E	T	U	J
S	F	O	J	U	D	C	T	E
E	J	B	T	O	C	S	F	U
T	C	U	S	E	F	B	J	O
U	O	C	E	S	S	J	B	F
J	T	S	B	F	F	E	O	C
F	B	E	O	C	C	U	S	T

Clue Word : SUBJECT OF   PUZZLE#44

G	E	R	P	O	T	T	I	N
T	P	R	E	I	N	G	O	R
I	N	O	G	R	R	E	T	P
O	R	I	T	N	G	P	R	E
E	R	T	O	P	R	I	N	G
N	G	P	R	E	I	T	R	O
R	O	E	R	T	P	N	G	I
P	T	N	I	G	O	R	E	R
R	I	G	N	R	E	O	P	T

Clue Word : REPORTING   PUZZLE#45

D	S	U	I	G	T	N	Y	A
I	N	Y	U	A	D	G	T	S
G	T	A	N	Y	S	D	I	U
Y	U	N	G	S	I	A	S	T
T	G	S	Y	U	A	I	D	N
A	D	I	T	S	N	U	G	Y
U	A	G	S	I	Y	T	N	D
N	Y	D	A	T	G	S	U	I
S	I	T	D	N	U	Y	A	G

Clue Word : STUDYING A   PUZZLE#46

E	I	O	T	M	U	H	L	B
T	B	M	E	L	H	O	U	I
H	U	L	L	B	O	E	T	M
M	O	H	H	E	L	I	B	T
U	L	I	I	H	T	M	O	E
B	E	T	T	O	I	U	H	L
L	M	U	U	I	B	T	E	H
O	H	E	E	T	M	B	I	U
I	T	B	B	U	E	L	M	O

Clue Word : BUILT HOME   PUZZLE#47

O	H	E	U	V	A	N	G	R
V	N	A	E	G	R	O	U	H
G	R	U	H	O	N	E	V	A
R	A	N	V	E	G	U	H	O
E	U	V	N	H	O	A	R	G
H	G	O	A	R	U	V	E	N
A	O	H	G	U	E	R	N	V
U	V	R	O	N	H	G	A	E
N	E	G	R	A	V	H	O	U

Clue Word : HUNG OVER A   PUZZLE#48

PUZZLE#49 — Clue Word : OUTBREAKS

B	E	K	A	O	T	R	S	V
R	S	A	U	E	B	O	K	T
T	U	O	R	S	K	A	E	B
E	B	T	K	R	O	U	A	S
S	A	R	T	U	E	B	O	K
K	O	U	S	B	A	T	R	E
O	R	S	E	T	U	K	B	A
U	K	E	B	A	R	S	T	O
A	T	B	O	K	S	E	U	R

PUZZLE#50 — Clue Word : 1754 THE

N	5	E	I	1	T	7	4	H
T	1	I	7	4	H	5	E	N
7	4	H	N	5	R	T	I	1
1	I	7	H	T	4	E	N	5
4	H	T	S	E	N	I	1	7
5	E	N	1	7	I	4	H	T
I	7	1	E	N	5	H	T	4
H	T	5	4	I	1	N	7	E
E	N	4	T	H	7	1	5	I

PUZZLE#51 — Clue Word : THE ALBANY

A	H	N	A	T	Y	E	B	L
E	Y	B	L	H	N	A	A	T
T	A	L	A	E	B	Y	H	N
Y	N	E	B	A	T	H	L	A
A	L	H	Y	N	E	A	T	B
B	A	T	H	A	L	N	E	Y
L	B	A	N	Y	H	T	A	E
H	T	Y	E	L	A	B	N	A
N	E	A	T	B	A	L	Y	H

PUZZLE#52 — Clue Word : OF THE PLAN

F	N	E	O	T	A	P	H	L
T	P	H	F	E	L	N	O	A
A	L	O	N	P	H	F	E	T
N	E	P	T	O	F	A	L	H
H	F	T	A	L	N	O	P	E
L	O	A	P	H	E	T	N	F
O	H	F	E	A	P	L	T	N
P	A	L	H	N	T	E	F	O
E	T	N	L	F	O	H	A	P

H	T	D	W	U	Y	O	L	E
W	U	Y	O	L	E	H	T	D
O	L	E	H	T	D	Y	W	U
E	D	L	T	H	W	U	Y	O
T	W	U	E	Y	O	D	H	L
Y	O	H	U	D	L	T	E	W
L	Y	O	D	E	H	W	U	T
U	E	W	Y	O	T	L	D	H
D	H	T	L	W	U	E	O	Y

Clue Word : THEY WOULD   PUZZLE#53

L	M	I	O	S	C	P	A	R
A	R	O	L	I	P	M	C	S
S	C	P	A	R	M	I	O	L
P	O	A	I	M	L	S	R	C
C	L	M	R	A	S	O	P	I
I	S	R	P	C	O	L	M	A
M	P	S	S	L	R	I	I	O
R	I	M	M	O	A	S	S	P
O	A	C	C	P	I	L	L	M

Clue Word : PROCLAIMS   PUZZLE#54

U	O	I	L	T	E	C	D	N
T	L	E	D	C	N	O	I	U
N	C	D	U	O	I	T	L	E
L	D	N	O	I	U	E	T	C
C	U	O	T	E	D	I	N	L
E	I	T	C	N	L	U	O	D
D	N	C	I	U	O	L	E	T
O	T	L	E	D	C	N	U	I
I	E	U	N	L	T	D	C	O

Clue Word : TO INCLUDE   PUZZLE#55

1	F	C	O	7	4	6	T	A
7	6	4	A	C	T	O	F	1
T	O	A	F	1	6	C	7	4
C	4	1	T	O	A	7	6	F
O	A	T	6	F	7	1	4	C
F	7	6	1	4	C	T	A	O
4	C	O	7	6	F	A	1	T
A	1	7	4	T	O	F	C	6
6	T	F	C	A	1	4	O	7

Clue Word : ACT OF 1764   PUZZLE#56

PUZZLE#57

6	A	T	5	7	O	1	F	C
O	F	5	C	1	6	T	A	7
7	C	1	F	A	T	6	5	O
C	1	F	A	6	5	O	7	T
A	O	7	1	T	C	5	6	F
T	5	6	7	O	F	A	C	1
1	7	O	6	F	A	C	T	5
5	T	A	O	C	7	F	1	6
F	6	C	T	5	1	7	O	A

Clue Word : ACT OF 1765

PUZZLE#58

S	C	E	M	N	T	O	U	D
T	U	D	E	O	C	M	N	S
N	O	M	S	U	D	T	E	C
U	D	T	O	M	S	N	C	E
E	N	O	D	C	U	S	M	T
M	S	C	N	T	E	U	D	O
O	M	S	C	D	N	E	T	U
C	E	U	T	S	M	D	O	N
D	T	N	U	E	O	C	S	M

Clue Word : DOCUMENTS

PUZZLE#59

O	S	A	E	R	L	T	I	N
T	L	I	N	O	A	E	S	R
E	R	N	S	I	T	A	L	O
R	I	O	T	E	N	L	A	S
A	N	E	I	L	S	R	O	T
S	T	L	R	A	O	N	E	I
N	O	S	A	T	E	I	R	L
L	A	R	O	N	I	S	T	E
I	E	T	L	S	R	O	N	A

Clue Word : RELATIONS

PUZZLE#60

F	7	C	7	O	A	T	3	1
7	A	T	F	3	1	O	7	C
3	O	1	C	7	T	A	7	F
T	F	O	1	A	7	3	C	7
A	7	7	O	C	3	F	1	T
1	C	3	T	7	F	7	A	O
7	T	7	A	F	C	1	O	3
O	3	F	7	1	7	C	T	A
C	1	1	3	T	O	7	F	7

Clue Word : ACT OF 1773

Q	L	K	O	I	T	Y	C	U
U	T	I	C	L	Y	K	O	Q
O	C	Y	U	K	Q	L	I	T
L	U	T	Q	Y	C	O	K	I
Y	K	Q	L	O	I	U	T	C
C	I	O	T	U	K	Q	Y	L
I	O	L	Y	T	U	C	Q	K
K	Y	C	I	Q	L	T	U	O
T	Q	U	K	C	O	I	L	Y

Clue Word : QUCIKLY TO   PUZZLE#61

F	O	4	1	T	C	A	7	7
1	T	A	F	7	7	C	O	4
7	7	C	O	4	A	T	1	F
T	4	F	A	1	7	7	C	O
A	7	7	4	C	O	F	T	1
C	1	O	T	7	F	4	7	A
7	A	7	C	F	1	O	4	T
O	C	T	7	A	4	1	F	7
4	F	1	7	O	T	7	A	C

Clue Word : ACT OF 1774   PUZZLE#62

S	A	O	O	P	T	J	M	R
J	T	P	P	O	M	A	S	E
M	R	E	E	J	A	T	P	O
P	O	T	T	S	E	M	R	A
E	M	R	R	A	O	S	T	J
A	J	S	S	M	R	E	O	P
T	E	A	A	R	S	P	J	M
R	S	J	J	E	P	O	A	T
O	P	M	M	T	J	R	E	S

Clue Word : MAJOR STEP   PUZZLE#63

3	N	O	7	A	T	1	8	D
A	8	T	1	D	3	7	O	N
1	D	7	N	O	8	3	A	T
O	A	1	3	T	D	8	N	7
D	7	8	A	1	N	O	T	3
N	T	3	O	8	7	D	1	A
8	3	D	T	N	1	A	A	O
7	O	N	8	3	A	T	T	1
T	1	A	D	7	O	N	N	8

Clue Word : TO 1783 AND   PUZZLE#64

A	N	F	G	O	G	D	E	U
O	D	G	F	E	U	G	A	N
G	E	U	N	A	D	O	G	F
G	G	D	U	N	O	E	F	A
F	U	E	D	G	A	N	G	O
N	O	A	E	F	G	U	D	G
D	A	G	O	U	F	G	B	E
U	G	N	A	D	E	F	O	G
E	F	O	G	G	N	A	U	D

Clue Word : GAGE FOUUD

PUZZLE#65

E	L	G	N	X	I	T	O	N
N	N	I	E	T	O	X	G	L
X	T	O	N	G	L	E	I	N
I	E	N	G	N	X	L	T	O
G	X	L	I	O	T	N	N	E
T	O	N	L	E	N	I	X	G
L	G	X	T	N	E	O	N	I
N	I	T	O	L	N	G	E	X
O	N	E	X	I	G	N	L	T

Clue Word : LEXINGTON

PUZZLE#66

R	O	E	I	N	G	A	D	Z
G	N	I	A	Z	D	O	E	R
A	Z	D	O	E	R	N	G	I
E	R	G	Z	I	N	D	O	A
I	A	O	G	D	E	Z	R	N
N	D	Z	R	A	O	G	I	E
Z	I	R	D	O	A	E	N	G
D	E	A	N	G	I	R	Z	O
O	G	N	E	R	Z	I	A	D

Clue Word : ORGANIZED

PUZZLE#67

C	Y	O	R	B	G	O	A	E
A	B	U	C	E	Y	G	R	U
G	E	R	U	A	O	Y	C	B
R	G	A	Y	U	C	B	B	O
Y	U	C	B	O	E	A	A	R
B	O	E	A	G	R	U	U	C
E	R	B	O	Y	A	C	C	G
O	A	G	E	C	U	R	R	Y
U	C	Y	G	R	B	E	E	A

Clue Word : BY COURAGE

PUZZLE#68

K	L	U	E	T	H	N	I	C
H	N	I	K	L	C	T	E	U
C	T	E	I	N	U	L	H	K
I	U	N	T	H	E	K	C	L
T	C	L	U	K	I	H	N	E
E	K	H	L	C	N	I	U	T
U	H	T	N	E	L	C	K	I
L	I	C	H	U	K	E	T	N
N	E	K	C	I	T	U	L	H

Clue Word : LUCK IN THE   PUZZLE#69

E	S	D	H	B	P	L	I	U
U	H	B	D	I	L	S	E	P
I	P	L	E	S	U	D	B	H
B	U	P	I	D	E	H	L	S
H	D	I	P	L	S	B	U	E
S	L	E	U	H	B	I	P	D
D	B	U	L	E	H	P	S	I
P	I	S	B	U	D	E	H	L
L	E	H	S	P	I	U	D	B

Clue Word : PUBLISHED   PUZZLE#70

E	L	R	I	G	D	C	A	N
I	N	G	L	A	C	R	D	E
A	D	C	N	E	R	I	L	G
C	I	L	G	N	A	D	E	R
R	E	D	C	I	L	N	G	A
G	A	N	D	R	E	L	I	C
L	C	A	E	D	N	G	R	I
N	R	E	A	L	G	E	C	D
D	G	I	R	C	I	A	N	L

Clue Word : DECCARING   PUZZLE#71

E	N	G	I	L	T	P	D	N
T	L	A	N	N	D	G	N	E
O	D	N	G	N	G	L	A	T
N	E	L	R	T	O	A	G	N
D	T	N	E	G	A	E	O	L
A	G	O	O	E	N	N	T	D
N	O	E	P	D	N	T	L	A
G	N	D	D	A	L	N	E	O
L	A	T	T	O	E	D	N	G

Clue Word : ENGLAND TO   PUZZLE#72

Puzzle #73

S	R	T	U	M	Y	O	H	A
Y	H	U	A	S	O	M	T	R
O	A	M	H	R	T	Y	U	S
T	M	H	Y	A	U	S	R	O
A	U	O	S	T	R	H	M	Y
R	Y	S	O	H	M	T	A	U
U	S	A	M	O	H	R	Y	T
M	O	R	T	Y	A	U	S	H
H	T	Y	R	U	S	A	O	M

Clue Word : ARMY SOUTH   PUZZLE#73

Puzzle #74

P	U	A	E	H	D	T	N	O
E	O	D	T	N	A	P	H	U
T	H	N	U	O	P	D	E	A
H	D	U	N	A	E	O	T	P
O	E	T	P	U	H	N	A	D
N	A	P	D	T	O	E	U	H
U	T	H	O	D	N	A	P	E
D	N	E	A	P	U	H	O	T
A	P	O	H	E	T	U	D	N

Clue Word : UPON DEATH   PUZZLE#74

Puzzle #75

C	D	A	N	H	E	O	R	M
N	E	O	M	R	C	H	D	A
H	R	M	O	D	A	C	N	E
O	M	R	E	C	D	A	H	N
D	C	H	A	O	N	M	E	R
A	N	E	H	M	R	D	C	O
E	O	D	D	N	M	R	A	H
R	H	N	N	A	O	E	M	C
M	A	C	C	E	H	N	O	D

Clue Word : MARCHED ON   PUZZLE#75

Puzzle #76

O	T	Q	G	R	M	U	U	I
N	R	U	Q	T	I	M	G	O
I	G	M	O	U	N	Q	T	R
M	U	O	N	I	R	G	Q	T
Q	I	G	U	O	T	R	M	N
T	N	R	M	G	Q	O	I	U
U	Q	I	T	M	O	N	R	G
R	O	N	I	Q	G	T	U	M
G	M	T	R	N	U	I	O	Q

Clue Word : QUOTTING MR   PUZZLE#76

PUZZLE#77

T	D	C	E	N	I	A	D	R
N	D	A	R	D	C	I	E	T
E	R	I	D	A	T	N	D	C
A	I	D	D	R	N	C	T	E
D	E	R	T	C	A	D	N	I
C	N	T	I	E	D	D	R	A
D	T	E	A	I	D	R	C	N
I	C	D	N	T	R	E	A	D
R	A	N	C	D	E	T	I	D

Clue Word : AND CREDIT

PUZZLE#78

W	S	W	I	N	H	A	T	O
N	A	T	O	W	S	I	H	W
O	I	H	W	A	T	W	N	S
I	O	A	H	W	W	T	S	N
W	N	W	T	S	O	H	I	A
T	G	S	A	I	N	O	W	W
S	W	P	W	T	I	N	A	J
H	T	N	S	O	A	W	W	I
A	W	I	N	H	W	S	O	T

Clue Word : WHAT IS NOW

PUZZLE#79

F	U	R	N	E	M	U	A	B
M	B	N	R	A	O	O	F	E
E	A	O	U	B	F	R	M	N
U	M	A	B	N	R	F	E	O
R	N	B	O	F	E	M	U	A
O	F	E	M	U	A	N	B	R
N	R	F	A	M	B	E	O	U
A	O	M	E	R	U	B	N	F
B	E	U	F	O	N	A	R	M

Clue Word : A NUMBER OF

PUZZLE#80

O	S	E	J	P	L	U	N	A
L	U	J	O	A	N	E	S	P
P	A	N	U	S	E	L	O	J
U	O	A	E	J	S	N	P	L
M	E	L	P	O	U	J	A	S
J	P	S	L	N	A	O	U	E
A	N	O	S	W	J	P	L	U
E	L	P	A	V	O	S	J	N
S	J	U	N	L	P	A	E	O

Clue Word : PAUL JONES

G	A	F	G	U	T	O	H	N
M	O	N	M	H	A	U	T	F
H	T	U	O	F	N	G	A	M
U	M	G	T	A	O	F	N	H
O	N	A	H	G	F	M	U	T
T	F	H	N	M	U	A	O	G
N	H	M	A	O	G	T	F	U
A	U	T	F	N	M	H	G	O
F	G	O	U	T	H	N	M	A

Clue Word : MAN FOUGHT   PUZZLE#81

M	0	Y	N	7	A	1	8	I
1	7	I	8	Y	0	N	A	M
8	N	A	M	1	I	Y	0	7
A	8	M	I	N	7	0	1	Y
0	1	N	A	M	Y	7	I	8
I	Y	7	0	8	1	A	M	N
Y	A	8	7	0	M	I	N	1
N	I	1	Y	A	8	M	7	0
7	M	0	1	I	N	8	Y	A

Clue Word : IN MAY 1780   PUZZLE#82

C	M	A	N	U	I	O	S	L
N	U	I	S	L	O	A	M	C
O	L	S	A	C	M	N	U	I
L	A	C	I	M	N	U	O	S
S	I	M	O	A	U	L	C	N
U	N	O	C	S	L	M	I	A
A	S	L	M	O	C	I	N	U
M	C	N	U	I	A	S	L	O
I	O	U	L	N	S	C	A	M

Clue Word : NO MUSICAL   PUZZLE#83

1	7	I	F	O	7	2	N	R
O	8	N	2	8	R	1	I	F
F	R	2	I	N	1	8	7	O
R	O	1	N	7	I	F	2	8
I	N	8	1	F	2	R	O	7
7	2	F	8	R	O	N	1	I
2	1	R	7	I	8	O	F	N
8	F	7	O	2	N	I	R	1
N	I	O	R	1	F	7	8	2

Clue Word : FOR IN 1782   PUZZLE#84

PUZZLE#85

U	E	N	G	R	I	H	D	T
R	D	T	E	N	H	U	G	I
H	I	G	T	D	U	E	N	R
T	G	D	R	E	N	I	H	U
E	R	H	U	I	G	D	T	N
I	N	U	D	H	T	R	E	G
N	H	R	I	G	D	T	U	E
G	T	I	H	U	E	N	R	D
D	U	E	N	T	R	G	I	H

Clue Word : DURING THE

PUZZLE#86

U	O	F	N	A	R	B	M	E
R	N	E	U	B	M	O	F	A
A	M	B	O	F	E	N	U	R
N	A	M	F	U	B	R	E	O
B	U	O	R	E	N	M	A	F
F	E	R	A	M	O	U	N	B
M	B	N	E	R	F	A	O	U
O	F	U	B	N	A	E	R	M
E	R	A	M	O	U	F	B	N

Clue Word : A NUMBER OF

PUZZLE#87

N	O	1	8	F	I	R	2	7
8	R	2	1	N	7	F	O	I
7	I	F	2	O	R	N	1	8
F	2	R	O	1	8	I	7	N
1	8	O	7	I	N	2	F	R
I	N	7	F	R	2	1	8	O
O	7	N	I	2	F	8	R	1
2	1	I	R	8	O	7	N	F
R	F	9	N	7	1	O	I	2

Clue Word : FOR IN 1782

PUZZLE#88

T	H	O	Y	C	E	U	S	L
C	U	E	H	D	L	T	Y	O
D	Y	L	U	T	O	H	E	V
Y	O	C	E	H	U	D	L	Y
L	E	U	T	Y	D	O	C	H
H	T	D	L	O	C	E	U	Y
O	L	T	D	U	Y	C	H	E
U	C	Y	O	E	H	L	T	D
E	D	H	C	L	T	Y	O	U

Clue Word : THEY COULD

N	H	G	C	F	R	O	E	A
R	O	F	N	A	E	C	H	G
A	E	C	H	O	G	F	N	R
H	A	E	G	C	F	N	R	O
O	G	N	E	R	H	A	C	F
C	F	R	A	N	O	E	G	H
G	R	O	F	E	C	H	A	N
E	N	H	O	G	A	R	F	C
F	C	A	R	H	N	G	O	E

Clue Word : FOR CHANGE   PUZZLE#89

F	A	O	N	L	T	P	H	E
N	P	L	E	F	H	T	O	A
H	T	E	O	A	P	F	N	L
P	H	F	L	T	O	E	A	N
A	E	T	F	H	N	L	P	O
O	L	N	A	P	E	H	F	T
E	O	P	H	N	L	A	T	F
L	F	H	T	O	A	N	E	P
T	N	A	P	E	F	O	L	H

Clue Word : OF THE PLAN   PUZZLE#90

M	Y	E	F	H	T	N	A	O
A	N	F	M	O	Y	H	E	T
H	T	O	E	N	A	M	Y	F
F	H	A	N	M	O	Y	T	E
O	M	T	Y	F	E	A	H	N
Y	E	N	T	A	H	F	O	M
T	A	M	O	Y	N	E	F	H
E	F	Y	H	T	M	O	N	A
N	O	H	A	E	F	T	M	Y

Clue Word : MANY OF THE   PUZZLE#91

U	A	I	S	Q	O	T	N	E
O	E	Q	U	T	N	S	A	I
T	S	N	E	A	I	O	U	Q
I	U	O	A	E	Q	N	T	S
A	T	S	N	I	U	E	Q	O
N	Q	E	O	S	T	A	I	U
Q	N	U	T	O	S	I	E	A
E	O	T	I	U	A	Q	S	N
S	I	A	Q	N	E	U	O	T

Clue Word : A QUESTION   PUZZLE#92

U	L	E	N	D	I	T	C	O
C	N	D	E	T	O	I	U	L
I	T	O	L	U	C	D	N	E
D	I	T	O	E	N	U	L	C
E	O	U	C	L	D	N	I	T
L	C	N	T	I	U	E	O	D
T	E	I	U	C	L	O	D	N
N	D	C	I	O	E	L	T	U
O	U	L	D	N	T	C	E	I

Clue Word : TO INCLUDE — PUZZLE#93

F	I	Y	U	C	H	T	E	D
U	C	D	T	F	E	H	I	Y
T	H	E	Y	I	D	C	U	F
C	T	H	F	D	U	E	Y	I
D	Y	U	C	E	I	F	T	H
I	E	F	H	T	Y	D	C	U
H	U	C	D	Y	T	I	F	E
E	D	T	I	U	F	Y	H	C
Y	F	I	E	H	C	U	D	T

Clue Word : CHIEF DUTY — PUZZLE#94

S	C	O	N	V	R	P	P	I
I	N	P	R	S	C	V	O	E
E	R	V	P	O	I	C	S	N
R	E	I	V	N	O	P	C	S
C	V	N	S	E	P	O	I	R
O	P	S	I	C	R	N	E	V
V	S	C	E	P	N	I	R	O
P	I	E	O	R	V	S	N	C
N	O	R	C	I	S	E	V	P

Clue Word : PROUINCES — PUZZLE#95

E	9	8	L	1	R	7	Y	A
L	R	A	Y	E	7	9	1	8
1	Y	7	A	9	8	E	L	R
8	7	L	9	R	E	Y	A	1
R	E	Y	7	A	1	8	9	L
A	1	9	8	Y	L	R	7	E
Y	9	E	1	L	9	A	R	7
9	L	R	E	7	A	1	8	Y
7	A	1	R	8	Y	L	E	9

Clue Word : EARLY 1789 — PUZZLE#96

Puzzle 97

O	S	R	P	E	I	A	F	T
P	I	E	A	F	T	S	O	R
F	A	T	O	R	S	E	P	I
S	T	F	R	P	O	I	A	E
E	R	P	F	I	A	O	T	S
A	O	I	S	T	E	F	R	P
T	E	A	I	O	P	R	S	F
I	F	S	T	A	R	P	E	O
R	P	O	E	S	F	T	I	A

Clue Word : PARTIES OF
PUZZLE#97

Puzzle 98

N	S	A	F	G	R	O	I	E
G	F	O	S	E	I	R	N	A
E	R	I	N	A	O	S	G	F
R	N	E	A	O	G	I	F	S
I	A	F	R	S	E	N	O	G
O	G	S	I	N	F	A	E	R
A	O	G	E	O	S	F	R	N
F	E	N	O	R	A	G	S	I
S	I	R	G	F	N	E	A	O

Clue Word : AS FOREIGN
PUZZLE#98

Puzzle 99

7	3	E	A	L	9	R	1	Y
A	1	Y	7	R	E	3	L	9
L	9	R	3	1	Y	7	E	A
E	Y	A	9	7	1	L	3	R
3	L	1	R	Y	A	E	9	7
R	7	9	E	3	L	A	Y	1
1	E	7	Y	A	3	9	R	L
Y	A	3	L	9	R	1	7	E
9	R	L	1	3	7	Y	A	3

Clue Word : EARLY 1793
PUZZLE#99

Puzzle 100

R	F	L	E	T	O	I	U	A
O	T	U	L	A	I	F	E	R
E	I	A	R	F	U	T	O	L
L	A	E	O	R	F	U	I	T
F	R	O	U	I	T	A	L	E
I	U	T	A	L	E	R	F	O
U	L	R	I	O	A	E	T	F
A	E	F	T	U	L	O	R	I
T	O	I	F	E	R	L	A	U

Clue Word : FAILURE TO
PUZZLE#100

S	O	U	R	A	E	B	T	K
K	B	R	U	T	S	E	O	A
A	E	T	B	O	K	U	R	S
R	S	O	K	E	A	T	U	B
U	A	K	O	B	T	R	S	E
E	T	B	S	U	R	K	A	O
B	K	S	T	R	O	A	E	U
T	U	A	E	S	B	O	K	R
O	R	E	A	K	U	S	B	T

Clue Word : OUT BREAKS   PUZZLE#101

F	Y	A	O	M	T	N	P	E
T	E	O	Y	N	P	F	A	M
M	N	P	F	A	E	Y	T	O
N	M	E	A	T	F	O	Y	P
Y	O	F	M	P	N	T	E	A
P	A	T	E	Y	O	M	N	F
E	P	Y	T	F	M	A	O	N
O	T	M	N	E	A	P	F	Y
A	F	N	P	O	Y	E	M	T

Clue Word : PAYMENT OF   PUZZLE#102

T	N	S	L	R	I	O	A	E
L	R	A	S	O	E	T	I	N
I	E	O	A	T	N	L	S	R
N	T	R	I	A	O	E	L	S
A	I	L	R	E	S	N	T	O
O	S	E	T	N	L	I	R	A
E	A	T	N	I	R	S	O	L
S	O	I	E	L	A	R	N	T
R	L	N	O	S	T	A	E	I

Clue Word : RELATIONS   PUZZLE#103

D	N	Z	H	T	E	A	X	Y
H	T	E	X	A	Y	N	Z	D
A	Y	X	Z	N	D	H	T	E
E	D	H	N	X	Z	Y	A	T
X	A	T	Y	D	H	Z	E	N
Y	Z	N	T	E	A	D	H	X
T	H	D	A	Y	X	E	N	Z
Z	X	Y	E	H	N	T	D	A
N	E	A	D	Z	T	X	Y	H

Clue Word : AND THE XYZ   PUZZLE#104

Y	N	T	R	A	D	E	O	P
E	R	D	P	O	N	T	A	Y
A	O	P	E	T	Y	D	N	R
P	D	R	N	Y	O	A	E	T
T	E	N	A	D	R	Y	P	O
O	Y	A	T	E	P	R	D	N
D	P	O	Y	R	A	N	T	E
N	T	Y	D	P	E	O	R	A
R	A	E	O	N	T	P	Y	D

Clue Word : DEPORT ANY   PUZZLE#105

I	N	A	O	S	R	G	H	T
T	S	H	G	I	A	R	N	O
R	G	O	N	H	T	I	A	S
N	I	R	S	O	G	H	T	A
H	T	S	A	R	I	O	G	N
A	O	G	T	N	H	S	R	I
G	H	N	I	A	O	T	S	R
O	A	T	R	G	S	N	I	H
S	R	I	H	T	N	A	O	G

Clue Word : RIGHTS ON A   PUZZLE#106

L	W	A	N	I	1	9	5	7
S	I	9	A	7	L	N	1	W
N	7	1	9	5	W	L	A	I
I	A	N	5	1	7	W	9	L
7	9	L	W	N	A	1	I	5
1	5	W	I	L	9	A	7	N
W	N	7	1	A	5	I	L	9
A	L	I	7	9	N	5	W	1
9	1	5	L	W	I	7	N	A

Clue Word : LAW IN 1795   PUZZLE#107

G	M	I	U	O	T	N	Q	R
O	Q	R	I	G	N	T	M	U
T	U	N	Q	M	R	G	O	I
M	N	O	G	Q	U	I	R	T
Q	I	U	T	R	O	M	G	N
R	T	G	M	N	I	Q	U	O
U	R	Q	N	I	G	O	T	M
I	G	T	O	U	M	R	N	Q
N	O	M	R	T	Q	U	I	G

Clue Word : QOUTING MR   PUZZLE#108

R	F	M	O	I	E	A	D	L
D	L	I	R	F	A	M	O	E
O	E	A	D	L	M	F	I	R
E	A	L	M	R	I	O	F	D
F	M	O	A	D	L	E	R	I
I	D	R	E	O	F	L	A	M
A	O	E	I	M	R	D	L	F
L	I	D	F	E	O	R	M	A
M	R	F	L	A	D	I	E	O

Clue Word : DILEMA FOR   PUZZLE#109

I	P	D	V	E	O	A	S	R
A	E	R	D	S	I	P	V	O
V	O	S	P	A	R	E	D	I
R	V	I	A	D	P	O	E	S
E	A	P	O	R	S	D	I	V
S	D	O	I	V	E	R	P	A
D	S	V	E	O	A	I	R	P
P	R	A	S	I	D	V	O	E
O	I	E	R	P	V	S	A	D

Clue Word : PROVIDES A   PUZZLE#110

H	L	E	U	T	I	P	C	B
U	I	T	B	C	P	E	L	H
B	C	P	E	L	H	U	I	T
C	E	I	L	P	T	H	B	U
T	P	H	C	B	U	I	E	L
L	B	U	I	H	E	C	T	P
I	U	B	P	E	L	T	H	C
P	H	C	T	I	B	L	U	E
E	T	L	H	U	C	B	P	I

Clue Word : THE PUBLIC   PUZZLE#111

E	R	U	Z	H	I	T	A	O
I	A	Z	O	R	T	E	U	H
O	T	H	E	U	A	Z	I	R
A	E	I	H	Z	R	U	O	T
T	H	O	A	E	U	R	Z	I
Z	U	R	I	T	O	H	E	A
H	O	E	R	A	Z	I	T	U
U	Z	A	T	I	H	O	R	E
R	I	T	U	O	E	A	H	Z

Clue Word : AUTHORIZE   PUZZLE#112

PUZZLE#113

L	E	C	S	O	T	A	N	I
O	S	A	N	L	I	T	E	C
N	T	I	E	A	C	L	O	S
C	L	O	T	S	A	N	I	E
T	A	E	I	N	O	C	S	L
I	N	S	C	E	L	O	T	A
A	C	N	O	I	S	E	L	T
S	O	L	A	T	E	I	C	N
E	I	T	L	C	N	S	A	O

Clue Word : COASTLINE

PUZZLE#114

P	H	R	A	S	U	C	D	E
D	C	S	P	R	E	A	U	H
E	A	U	C	D	H	P	S	S
H	P	D	E	A	R	S	C	U
S	R	C	H	U	P	D	E	A
A	U	E	D	C	S	H	R	P
R	D	A	U	H	C	E	P	S
U	E	H	S	P	D	R	A	C
C	S	P	R	E	A	U	H	D

Clue Word : PURCHASED

PUZZLE#115

O	W	L	E	C	A	I	R	P
R	P	C	I	W	L	A	O	E
A	I	E	O	R	P	L	W	C
E	O	A	L	I	R	P	C	W
I	C	W	P	O	E	R	A	L
L	R	P	C	A	W	O	E	I
P	L	R	A	E	C	W	I	O
C	A	I	W	L	O	E	P	R
W	E	O	R	P	I	C	L	A

Clue Word : LOW A PRICE

PUZZLE#116

L	X	R	N	P	G	E	I	O
O	E	I	R	X	L	N	P	G
N	G	P	E	I	O	R	X	L
G	I	O	X	N	P	L	E	R
R	L	E	O	G	I	P	N	X
X	P	N	L	E	R	G	O	I
P	O	L	I	R	E	X	G	N
E	R	X	G	O	N	I	L	P
I	N	G	P	L	X	O	R	E

Clue Word : EXPLORING

D	O	L	A	S	T	E	F	R
A	F	R	L	D	R	T	S	O
E	S	T	O	R	F	D	A	L
L	E	D	S	T	A	R	O	F
R	T	S	F	O	D	A	L	E
O	A	F	E	L	R	S	T	D
T	L	E	D	A	O	F	R	S
F	R	O	T	E	S	L	D	A
S	D	A	R	F	L	O	E	T

Clue Word : LASTED FOR   PUZZLE#117

N	H	V	T	Y	S	A	E	U
E	Y	A	V	U	N	H	S	T
T	S	U	H	A	E	V	N	Y
S	U	T	N	V	Y	E	H	A
H	A	Y	E	S	T	U	V	N
V	E	N	A	H	U	T	Y	S
A	T	E	S	N	H	Y	U	V
U	N	H	Y	T	V	S	A	E
Y	V	S	U	E	A	N	T	H

Clue Word : THE US NAVY   PUZZLE#118

U	E	D	N	G	I	R	H	T
H	I	G	T	D	R	E	U	N
T	R	N	U	H	E	D	I	G
E	U	T	H	I	D	G	N	R
N	H	R	G	E	T	I	D	U
G	D	I	R	U	N	T	E	H
R	G	E	D	N	H	U	T	I
I	T	H	E	R	U	N	G	D
D	N	U	I	T	G	H	R	E

Clue Word : DURING THE   PUZZLE#119

A	Y	C	P	B	U	E	T	R
T	E	U	Y	A	R	C	P	B
P	B	R	T	C	E	Y	U	A
B	U	Y	E	T	A	R	C	P
E	C	T	B	R	P	U	A	Y
R	A	P	C	U	Y	T	B	E
Y	R	B	U	P	T	A	E	C
C	T	E	A	Y	B	P	R	U
U	P	A	R	E	C	B	Y	T

Clue Word : CAPTURE BY   PUZZLE#120

U	P	I	E	S	T	G	V	A
E	T	S	A	V	G	P	I	U
V	G	A	U	P	I	S	E	T
A	I	E	G	T	U	V	S	P
G	U	V	P	I	S	T	A	E
T	S	P	V	A	E	I	U	G
P	V	G	I	U	A	E	T	S
S	E	U	T	G	V	A	P	I
I	A	T	S	E	P	U	G	V

Clue Word : GAVE UP ITS   PUZZLE#121

I	O	F	B	G	R	E	D	A
E	D	R	A	O	F	B	I	G
A	B	G	E	I	D	O	F	R
R	E	D	I	A	B	F	G	O
F	I	A	G	D	O	R	B	E
O	G	B	R	F	E	I	A	D
B	F	E	D	R	A	G	O	O
D	R	I	O	B	G	A	E	E
G	A	O	F	E	I	D	R	R

Clue Word : BRIGADE OF   PUZZLE#122

C	L	K	O	A	D	B	E	T
O	A	E	C	B	T	L	D	K
B	T	D	E	K	L	A	C	O
T	O	A	L	D	K	E	B	C
K	E	B	T	C	A	D	O	L
D	C	L	B	O	E	T	K	A
A	D	O	K	T	B	C	L	E
L	K	T	D	E	C	O	A	B
E	B	C	A	L	O	K	T	D

Clue Word : BLOCKED AT   PUZZLE#123

Y	H	R	T	A	1	9	E	L
E	T	L	Y	H	9	A	R	1
9	A	1	E	R	L	T	H	Y
T	R	9	L	E	Y	H	1	A
1	Y	E	H	9	A	L	T	R
H	L	A	R	1	T	E	Y	9
R	1	T	9	L	E	Y	A	H
L	E	H	A	Y	R	1	9	T
A	9	Y	1	T	H	R	L	E

Clue Word : EARLY 19TH   PUZZLE#124

L	N	O	I	A	M	T	P	C
C	T	I	L	N	P	A	M	O
A	M	P	O	T	C	N	I	L
N	A	M	T	P	L	O	C	I
O	I	C	A	M	N	L	T	P
T	P	L	C	I	O	M	A	N
M	C	N	P	L	A	I	O	T
I	O	A	N	C	T	P	L	M
P	L	T	M	O	I	C	N	A

Clue Word : COMPLAINT   PUZZLE#125

R	A	O	T	N	E	C	I	D
T	D	I	A	C	O	R	E	N
E	C	N	I	D	R	T	A	O
C	R	D	O	I	A	N	T	E
A	I	T	C	E	N	O	D	R
O	N	E	D	R	T	A	C	I
N	O	C	E	T	I	D	R	A
I	T	A	R	O	D	E	N	C
D	E	R	N	A	C	I	O	T

Clue Word : A DOCTRINE   PUZZLE#126

U	R	N	G	T	D	H	I	E
I	E	H	R	U	N	G	T	D
D	G	T	H	I	E	R	U	N
G	I	U	E	R	T	N	D	H
T	N	D	U	H	G	I	E	R
R	H	E	N	D	I	T	G	U
H	T	G	D	E	R	U	N	I
E	U	I	T	N	H	D	R	G
N	D	R	I	G	U	E	H	T

Clue Word : DURING THE   PUZZLE#127

T	A	L	E	O	H	S	W	D
E	O	S	W	D	A	L	T	H
H	W	D	T	L	S	A	E	O
A	T	E	E	S	L	O	H	W
S	D	W	W	E	O	T	A	L
L	H	O	O	W	T	D	S	E
O	L	H	H	A	W	E	D	T
W	E	A	A	T	D	H	L	S
D	S	T	T	H	E	W	O	A

Clue Word : WAS THE OLD   PUZZLE#128

O	I	A	E	S	R	N	G	W
E	G	S	W	N	A	O	R	I
R	W	N	I	G	O	S	A	E
N	S	R	O	A	W	I	E	G
I	A	W	N	E	G	R	O	S
G	O	E	R	I	S	W	N	A
A	E	I	S	O	N	G	W	R
S	R	O	G	W	E	A	I	N
W	N	G	A	R	I	E	S	O

Clue Word : REGION WAS　　　　　　　PUZZLE#129

E	7	9	A	F	0	1	T	R
A	F	T	R	1	E	7	0	9
O	R	1	T	9	7	E	A	F
1	0	R	E	7	T	9	F	A
T	E	7	F	A	9	O	R	1
9	A	F	1	O	R	T	E	7
R	T	A	7	E	1	F	9	0
F	1	0	9	T	A	R	7	E
7	9	E	0	R	F	A	1	T

Clue Word : AFTER 1790　　　　　　　PUZZLE#130

O	N	D	E	A	Z	G	I	R
R	A	E	O	G	I	N	D	Z
Z	I	G	R	N	D	O	A	E
N	D	R	A	Z	O	I	E	G
E	O	I	G	D	N	Z	R	A
G	Z	A	I	E	R	D	O	N
A	E	O	N	I	G	R	Z	D
D	R	N	Z	O	E	A	G	I
I	G	Z	D	R	A	E	N	O

Clue Word : ORGANIZED　　　　　　　PUZZLE#131

T	A	D	O	L	H	F	N	E
O	L	H	E	N	F	D	T	A
N	E	F	D	T	A	H	O	L
H	T	A	L	O	N	E	D	F
L	O	N	F	E	D	T	A	H
D	F	E	H	A	T	O	L	N
F	N	T	A	H	O	L	E	D
A	H	L	T	D	E	N	F	O
E	D	O	N	F	L	A	H	T

Clue Word : OF THE LAND　　　　　　　PUZZLE#132

Z	N	R	G	O	A	D	E	I
O	G	I	N	D	E	R	Z	A
A	E	D	I	R	Z	O	G	N
G	R	Z	O	A	D	I	N	E
D	O	N	Z	E	I	G	A	R
I	A	E	R	G	N	Z	O	D
R	Z	A	D	N	O	E	I	G
N	D	O	E	I	G	A	R	Z
E	I	G	A	Z	R	N	D	O

Clue Word : ORGANIZED   PUZZLE#133

V	H	M	I	L	U	E	C	D
D	U	C	M	E	H	I	V	L
L	E	I	D	C	V	H	U	M
U	I	E	C	V	M	L	D	H
H	V	L	U	D	E	M	I	C
M	C	D	H	I	L	U	E	V
I	L	V	E	M	C	D	H	U
E	M	H	V	U	D	C	L	I
C	D	U	L	H	I	V	M	E

Clue Word : LIUED MUCH   PUZZLE#134

R	E	D	C	N	S	A	O	U
A	C	S	D	O	U	N	R	E
N	O	U	A	R	E	D	S	C
C	R	A	U	E	D	S	N	O
D	U	N	O	S	R	E	C	A
O	S	E	N	A	C	R	U	D
U	N	R	E	D	O	C	A	S
S	D	O	R	C	A	U	E	N
E	A	C	S	U	N	O	D	R

Clue Word : AND SOURCE   PUZZLE#135

A	I	M	R	N	G	P	F	U
P	R	G	I	F	U	M	N	A
N	F	U	A	M	P	I	G	R
F	M	R	P	I	N	U	A	G
I	U	A	M	G	R	F	P	N
G	N	P	U	A	F	R	I	M
U	A	F	G	R	I	N	M	P
R	G	N	F	P	M	A	U	I
M	P	I	N	U	A	G	R	F

Clue Word : UP FARMING   PUZZLE#136

F	E	A	O	R	I	C	T	S
O	R	C	T	S	E	A	F	I
I	S	T	A	F	C	O	E	R
E	A	R	F	C	S	I	O	T
S	F	O	E	I	T	R	A	C
C	T	I	R	O	A	E	S	F
T	O	S	C	E	R	F	I	A
A	C	F	I	T	O	S	R	E
R	I	E	S	A	F	T	C	O

Clue Word : FACTORIES   PUZZLE#137

I	R	N	H	M	E	Y	C	A
E	H	M	A	C	Y	N	I	R
Y	A	C	I	N	R	E	H	M
C	I	R	N	Y	H	M	A	E
M	N	Y	E	A	I	C	R	H
H	E	A	M	R	C	I	N	Y
N	C	E	R	H	M	A	Y	I
A	M	H	Y	I	N	R	E	C
R	Y	I	C	E	A	H	M	N

Clue Word : MACHINERY   PUZZLE#138

T	O	N	I	H	A	P	S	D
H	A	P	D	O	S	I	N	T
S	I	D	N	P	T	A	O	H
P	T	A	S	I	D	S	H	O
D	H	O	A	N	P	N	T	I
I	N	S	H	T	O	D	A	P
N	P	T	P	A	I	H	D	S
A	D	I	T	S	N	O	P	N
O	S	H	P	D	H	T	I	A

Clue Word : AND TO SHIP   PUZZLE#139

T	R	N	U	S	K	E	I	P
U	P	I	E	N	T	S	R	K
K	E	S	I	R	P	U	N	T
E	N	U	S	K	I	P	T	R
S	T	K	N	P	R	I	U	E
P	I	R	T	U	E	K	S	N
N	S	T	K	E	U	R	P	I
I	K	P	R	T	S	N	E	U
R	U	E	P	I	N	T	K	S

Clue Word : TURN PIKES   PUZZLE#140

W	Y	T	O	E	L	G	D	I
E	L	G	D	W	I	Y	O	T
D	O	I	Y	T	G	E	W	L
L	T	Y	I	G	W	D	E	O
G	I	W	E	D	O	T	L	Y
O	E	D	T	L	Y	I	G	W
I	W	E	L	Y	D	O	T	G
Y	D	L	G	O	T	W	I	E
T	G	O	W	I	E	L	Y	D

Clue Word : GO WIDELY   PUZZLE#141

W	L	D	E	O	S	R	T	H
O	T	S	R	L	H	W	E	D
H	R	E	T	D	W	S	L	O
S	D	H	L	W	R	T	O	E
R	W	T	D	E	O	L	H	S
E	O	L	H	S	T	D	W	R
T	E	W	S	H	D	O	R	L
L	S	R	O	T	E	H	D	W
D	H	O	W	R	L	E	S	T

Clue Word : THE WORLDS   PUZZLE#142

R	G	E	A	S	B	M	Y	N
B	A	N	M	Y	E	S	G	R
M	S	Y	G	R	N	A	E	B
Y	E	R	N	B	S	G	A	M
N	M	S	E	G	A	R	B	Y
G	B	A	Y	M	R	E	N	S
S	Y	M	B	A	G	N	R	E
A	U	B	R	E	M	Y	S	G
E	R	G	S	N	Y	B	M	A

Clue Word : BY GERMANS   PUZZLE#143

8	U	1	N	T	2	I	B	4
T	4	I	8	1	B	2	U	N
N	2	B	4	I	U	8	1	T
B	T	2	1	4	I	N	8	U
U	I	8	B	N	T	1	4	2
1	N	4	U	2	8	T	I	B
4	B	N	T	8	1	U	2	I
2	1	T	I	U	4	B	N	8
I	8	U	2	B	N	4	T	1

Clue Word : IN 1824 BUT   PUZZLE#144

PUZZLE#145

A	7	8	1	F	9	T	R	E
E	F	R	7	A	T	1	8	9
9	1	T	8	R	E	F	7	A
8	T	9	R	E	7	A	1	F
F	A	E	T	8	1	R	9	7
7	E	1	F	9	A	E	T	8
R	E	F	9	1	8	7	A	T
1	8	7	A	T	F	9	E	R
T	9	A	E	7	R	8	F	1

Clue Word : AFTER 1789

PUZZLE#146

A	D	S	E	R	T	M	C	O
E	R	T	C	O	M	S	D	A
O	M	C	S	D	A	E	R	T
D	C	E	T	S	R	A	O	M
R	S	A	O	M	D	T	E	C
T	O	M	A	C	E	D	S	R
M	T	R	D	E	O	C	A	S
C	E	O	M	A	S	R	T	D
S	A	D	R	T	C	O	M	E

Clue Word : DEMOCRATS

PUZZLE#147

R	T	M	A	D	E	S	I	H
I	A	D	S	M	H	E	T	R
E	H	S	I	R	T	M	A	D
H	S	E	D	A	R	I	M	T
T	D	R	M	E	I	H	S	A
M	I	A	H	T	S	R	D	E
A	E	I	T	H	M	D	R	D
D	M	H	R	S	A	T	E	I
S	R	T	E	I	D	A	H	M

Clue Word : HARDTIMES

PUZZLE#148

M	O	E	W	L	T	N	H	I
T	W	N	O	H	I	M	L	E
H	I	L	M	E	N	O	T	W
L	E	H	T	I	M	W	N	O
O	N	T	L	W	E	H	I	M
I	M	W	N	O	H	T	E	L
N	L	O	E	T	W	I	M	H
W	T	I	H	M	L	E	O	N
E	H	M	I	N	O	L	W	T

Clue Word : NOW LET HIM

PUZZLE #149

L	P	B	C	N	U	A	I	D
C	A	I	B	D	L	N	U	P
N	U	D	A	I	P	L	C	B
I	B	A	N	L	C	D	P	U
U	N	P	I	B	D	C	L	A
D	L	C	U	P	A	B	N	I
B	D	N	P	C	I	U	A	L
A	I	L	D	U	N	P	B	C
P	C	U	L	A	B	I	D	N

Clue Word : PUBLIC AND

PUZZLE #150

M	L	R	T	O	P	F	I	S
T	S	O	M	I	F	R	P	L
F	P	I	L	S	R	M	T	O
O	R	F	P	M	I	L	S	T
P	I	L	S	F	T	O	R	M
S	M	T	O	R	L	P	F	I
I	O	P	R	L	S	T	M	F
R	F	M	I	T	O	S	L	P
L	T	S	F	P	M	I	O	R

Clue Word : SPLIT FROM

PUZZLE #151

G	C	D	H	E	Y	A	N	B
E	A	Y	D	N	B	G	H	C
N	B	H	C	G	A	D	E	Y
B	Y	A	E	D	N	H	C	G
D	H	E	A	C	G	Y	B	N
C	N	G	Y	B	H	E	D	A
Y	G	C	N	H	D	B	A	E
H	E	B	G	A	C	N	Y	D
A	D	N	B	Y	E	C	G	H

Clue Word : CHANGED BY

PUZZLE #152

C	T	O	I	E	V	A	N	D
A	N	I	D	T	C	E	O	U
U	D	E	A	N	O	I	T	C
T	C	U	O	A	E	D	I	N
N	I	A	U	D	T	C	E	O
O	E	D	N	C	I	U	A	T
E	A	N	T	U	D	O	C	I
D	O	T	C	I	A	N	U	E
I	U	C	E	O	N	T	D	A

Clue Word : EDUCATION